W9-CND-532

LONG
STROKES
IN A SHORT SEASON

Art Aungst
Total Immersion Coach

Total Immersion, Inc.
New Paltz, NY

ISBN: 1-931009-02-3

Long Strokes in a Short Season

Copyright ©2003 by Art Aungst. All rights reserved. No part of this book may be reproduced or transmitted in any form or by any means electronic or mechanical, including photocopying, printing, recording, or by any information storage and retrieval system, without permission in writing from Total Immersion, Inc. For information, contact: Total Immersion, Inc., 171 Main Street, New Paltz, NY 12561, Or e-mail: info@totalimmersion.net.

Text and concept: Art Aungst
Editing: Terry Laughlin and Jessica Aungst
Production: Tara Laughlin

Published by Total Immersion, Inc.
171 Main Street
New Paltz, NY 12561

For information about Terry Laughlin's books and Total Immersion swim workshops, visit our website at www.totalimmersion.net or call 800-609-7946 (845-256-9770 from outside the USA).

First edition published 2003
Printed in the United States of America

10 9 8 7 6 5 4 3 2 1

Acknowledgments

In memory of Tommie Gardner, Gene Mills and Jenna Kern who taught us so much about sport in their short time with us.

I would like to thank all of the swimmers I have had the privilege of coaching over the years who taught me so much about swimming and more importantly about life. Terry Laughlin for forcing me to believe I could ever write a book and for his help, support and unselfish donation of his time and advice. Barb Tomchin who was such a great coach to me. My kids, Becca, Molly, Judd, and especially Jessica, who so patiently edited. They always understood why daddy spent so much time raising other people's children.

Special thanks to my wife who has always made my swimmers part of her own family. Her understanding, patience and unwavering support made this possible.

CONTENTS

Foreword

Two years ago I got the idea to ask one of the Total Immersion coaches to write a book on real-time coaching, using TI methods. While some people still think of TI as mainly "a set of stroke drills," dozens of coaches currently using TI methods with their teams are finding it to be a complete framework and guide for every aspect of coaching competitive swimmers. And, in every instance, they report that their teams have swum much faster, achieved far more success and enjoyed the process far more than they had with traditional methods. The best way to show curious coaches and others how to coach a team "the TI way" would be a season-long, day-by-day journal by one of these coaches – including sample practices each week – with explanation of why they made the choices they did. Peeking "over the shoulder" of a successful coach would obviously teach you far more than reading a dry "text" about swimming theory.

After some thought I decided that Art Aungst would be perfect for this project. First, though he had never attempted a book, I knew that anything he wrote would be entertaining and engaging. He had written several articles for our on-line newsletter and several hundred email messages to me. So often he managed to be laugh-out-loud funny – how often do you laugh out loud while reading? – while making compelling arguments about swimming intelligently.

Second, he coaches a high school team with a 12-week season, giving him only 50 practices to transform his athletes into championship caliber swimmers – which he manages to do with stunning consistency: Over the past six years his girls have never finished lower than second in any relay (18 total relay races!) at the NY State Championships. The brevity of his season allows for a concise and highly focused picture of how to coach a swim team from first practice through taper and final race. As you will read, he does it in non-traditional, yet utterly logical ways. If the object of swim training is to prepare swimmers to maximize their racing potential – rather than condition them to do yet more training – you'll wonder why everyone doesn't do it Art's way.

What Art has written so far exceeded anything that I hoped for that I hardly know how to describe it. While Art tells you exactly how he coaches with such success, that is the least of its virtues. Long Strokes has breadth and depth, humanity and universality. No matter how faint your interest in coaching or swimming, I promise you'll be affected and instructed by virtually every page, just as I was 30 years ago by a book that Art cites several times – *Zen and the Art of Motorcycle Maintenance.*

If you're a swimming coach you'll learn how to make practice a place that swimmers enjoy coming to – you'll also learn how to teach essential skills like racing stroke rates. If you're an athlete you'll learn how to be a smarter and more informed swimmer – you'll also learn how to balance life outside the pool with that inside it. If you're a parent, you'll learn how sports experiences can be made to yield priceless life lessons. If you're an educator, you'll learn how to create an environment where learning becomes inevitable. Are you none of the above but simply curious about living a more examined and meaningful life? If so, you'll be both entertained and elevated by every chapter that follows.

And yet this is still a book about swimming and coaching intelligently and holistically. If fact, it is the best book on swimming I have ever had the privilege to read. I am intensely proud to publish it.

Terry Laughlin

Introduction

"When the Going gets weird, the weird turn pro."
-Hunter Thompson

It was one of the band's better nights.

Here it was 1a.m. and we had just finished the 3rd set.

It might have been that the crowd that night really dug us or that they had bad aim or that we were just getting better at ducking, but none of the beer bottles they had thrown had actually hit us. We were in the zone. It was a virtual certainty that we were going to "go the distance," and reach our goal of playing all four sets before we got fired.

I could see through the Camel smoke haze that she was looking at me.

It might have been the strength of those Hendrix-like licks on the pulsing polkas I lay down or the way those lederhosen showed off my knees, but there were few women who could resist the charms of us accordion players.

Having attention lavished on me by gorgeous women was just a thing I had become accustomed to — a part of the job — but this one was really special.

As I sauntered on over (my friend Terry keeps telling me it's important to never look like you're making an effort), I cocked my hat at a jaunty angle, making sure that the big red feather was just so. I realized this one would need my best opening line. I had to act and act fast, because the owners usually got full bore surly when they realized we had driven off most of the paying customers, and quick exits were always the order of the night.

I said, "Look baby, you don't know who you're talking to. I'm a high school swim coach!!!"

As the story progressed, the particular target of my attention was duly unimpressed with that fact.

I know this doesn't sound like the opening of a swimming book, but these were the first words I wrote when I started this project. Terry Laughlin had talked me into writing a book about technique-based short season swimming. I have had a great deal of experience with technique-based coaching and no experience with writing a book, so I did what I always did in high school and college when I had no clue as to how to proceed — I tried to bluff my way through with a bit of humor. I know myself well enough to understand that this was my way of dealing with the tremendous anxiety at the prospect of writing a book knowing full well that most of my friends and colleagues would be surprised to find that I had even ever read one.

As the season and writing progressed, I started to realize that while much of what I was writing about was extremely specific, a successful technique-based season is as much about attitude as anything. As I started to relax more and let things happen, the writing became easier. I realized that the anxiety I was feeling was exactly the same as I felt in 1997, when I radically changed the way I coached.

(Oh yeah, in case you are wondering, I don't really play an accordion. I really was in a band, though, and we did get fired frequently. And, yes, I am great at duly unimpressing women).

Rethinking My Coaching Beliefs

In the early 1990's, I heard Bill Boomer speak at numerous clinics. His message was that coaches have always focused on propulsion and training; he urged us to consider balancing the usual focus on "building the engine and fuel tank" with a focus on reshaping the vessel to make the available power and energy go further.

I began to incorporate his ideas into my practices, and we swam better than ever. Most striking, I could finally see my less-talented swimmers starting to look like naturals in the water. I was stunned to see that what I had always assumed was an inborn talent to move well through the water could actually be taught! As they began to look more fluent, the contributions of "average swimmers" to our success increased markedly as well. Yet, many of Boomer's ideas were still so elusive to me that I had difficulty transmitting them to my swimmers. I also had a hard time letting go of the idea that conditioning was the primary goal of a workout — much of my instruction consisted of me yelling to kids to lengthen and roll, but by god make the intervals.

Putting Belief into Practice

In 1996, I read Terry Laughlin's original Total Immersion book, and was struck by the simple and practical way it presented ideas similar to Boomer's. In my initial experiments with his ideas that fall, it proved to be not only a way to refine fundamentals but also provided opportunities for countless creative avenues to make practice challenging and fun. In addition, skills that previously took me a whole season to teach were mastered quickly — an essential in high school swimming, where the season lasts only 12 weeks. My initial experiences convinced me to remake our program from the ground up. Five years later that rebuilding is still a work in progress.

In my view, Terry's writing is the definitive work on a practical approach to better swimming. I feel strongly that any individual who religiously practices the drills that Total Immersion has developed over the years will become a better swimmer. The problem that I had in writing this book was that using these techniques and drills with a team was largely uncharted waters. I started to realize that there could be no definitive book on short season swimming, because each situation is vastly different in terms of pool time, talent levels, and length of season.

This book is a real-time chronicle of the Fall, 2001 season at Orchard Park High School, a diary of what my swimmers and I did week by week and the insights and lessons revealed by our experiences. I hope that our experiences may provide useful ideas for coaches, swimmers, parents, or anyone interested in the swimming-improvement process. I also hope that in addition to finding some possible solutions to problems faced in a short season, it will leave readers with the certainty that they can take ideas found here and customize them to arrive at better solutions for particular circumstances.

I have coached swimming at Orchard Park High School since 1983 and have been fortunate to have one of the most consistently successful teams in New York State. During this time, my teams have lost only five dual meets to other teams in our division. We've had Conference champions, Sectional champs, State champs, and All Americans.

I did a good job coaching kids with talent — swimmers who would have been good no matter who coached them. Yet, for all our "success," it always nagged at me that my success rate with less talented or less experienced kids was abysmal. To me, the real appeal of coaching is that I am first and foremost a teacher; my pool should be the ultimate classroom, because there I have nothing but bright, motivated kids who are with me of their own volition.

Workout vs. Practice

As we began the 1997 season, I told my team: "Last year we had our best season ever, but now we're going to do things differently. We have always prided ourselves on how hard we work, but from now on it's going to be about how right. We're going to stop 'training' and begin 'practicing'!!"

The difference is subtle but important, but getting in the habit of making sure I titled each day's events as a practice with the implication that the primary focus would be on skill acquisition helped me a great deal as a coach.

A technique-intensive approach has produced more enjoyment and satisfaction for me and my swimmers. Writing workouts was often a mundane chore. Now, writing practices is an exercise in creativity. I've seen that swimmers are much more intrinsically motivated to plunge into multidimensional tasks than to simply splash back and forth in varying degrees of discomfort or boredom. They are vocally enthused about coming to "practice" to a degree unknown when I ran "workouts."

Because of our significant improvement over the past four seasons, other high school coaches often inquire what our "secret" is. When I tell them that a "big" training day for us might be 4500 yards — most of it done slowly and precisely — they usually seem skeptical. Besides the conventional coaches' intuition that "more and harder" is the only way to swim faster, one of the things that might be a bit frightening to some of them is that a technique-based approach puts the burden of success squarely on the coach. In a technique-oriented program, it is the coach's job to provide specific focal points for every set so that swimmers are constantly challenged to think about excellence in each repetition (with the benefit that the more thought devoted to technique in practice, the less need there is for thought in a meet under pressure and fatigue).

In traditional training mode, it is the coach's job to establish proper workouts, and if this is done and the swimmer doesn't do well, she either didn't train hard enough or just doesn't have the talent. Talented kids will almost always respond to training, but as talent levels diminish, so does the value of traditional training.

Reaping Maximum Value from the High School "Talent Pool"

The unusual degree to which we have been able to create success based on significant contributions from athletes who don't consider themselves "swimmers" has been exciting for me to witness. Swimming misses out on a great deal of potential, because it typically holds little appeal for the person who has multiple athletic talents. The good athletes often look at swimming as mainly about "how much pain and tedium can you endure?" They ask, "Why should I endure that when I could be playing a game instead?"

By changing our program from how-far-and-how-hard to a constantly evolving set of challenges involving balance, self-awareness, and exploration of efficiency, we have greatly increased its appeal to a person's general athleticism.

The "buzz" this has generated around the school has translated into more good athletes from other sports who view swimming as a favorable choice for off-season.

Many kids who play volleyball, football, or soccer also play baseball, run track, and play lacrosse in other seasons. Many have outstanding athleticism that could be applied to swimming during a 12-week high school season if they were given the maximum opportunity to apply their athletic talents in the water. By making swimming more appealing through teaching, we have attracted many more of these kids to swim with us. By focusing on teaching and practice, rather than generic training, we have also given them the opportunity to swim quite fast in a brief season, and they have been instrumental to our success.

Results

In 1997, we had our best season to that point. We placed six girls who also play lacrosse, softball, and run track in state finals. They hit All American cuts in all three relays (though we could only submit the medley relay for recognition because we had a 7th grader — who made state finals in the 50 free — on the two freestyle relays). Our swimmers were beating kids who train all year following just 12 weeks of practice! More importantly, every girl on our team got much better.

In the period from 1996-2002, we had three relays in every state meet.

No other team has ever won all three relays.

	1998	**1999**	**2000**	**2001**	**2002**
200 Medley	1st	1st	1st	1st	2nd
200 Free	2nd	1st	2nd	2nd	1st
400 Free	4th	1st	2nd	2nd	2nd

In 2001 and 2002 we broke the state record in the 400 free and finished second to Newburgh.

In terms of time, it might be appropriate to compare results from our school records in all three relays from the 15 years when I emphasized training with the four seasons when I focused on teaching.

	1983-1997	**1998-2001**
200 Medley	1:52.95	1:49.95
200 Free	1:39.67	1:37.05 (state record)
400 Free	3:39.47	3:32.99
State Championship Events Won:	Two	Nine

Since 1998, I have had far fewer year-round swimmers than in the past, yet we are swimming far faster on far less training. This year's seniors have been defeated in only one dual meet and won four consecutive Conference titles during their years on the team.

Since moving to a more technique-based program in 1997, our boys' team has lost only two dual meets, and those were to the eventual State champions. In 1998 at States, we won the 200 free relay and finished second in the 400. We also had individual champions in the 100 back and 100 fly. We had an all-league volleyball player who swam only during the 12-week high school season finish 2nd in the 100 and 5th in the 50 free. In 1999, despite graduating two All Americans, we moved up to 1st in the 400 free relay at the State meet. We also beat Pittsford, the #1 team in the state, to end their three-year dual meet unbeaten streak. Again, a different all-league volleyball player provided us with critical points.

What I Have Learned from Coaching Differently

In talking to and observing other coaches, it is quite clear that our approach is unconventional. Most high school coaches attend clinic after clinic to learn more about how to train their swimmers. At those clinics, they hear of elaborate plans employing macro- and meso-cycles over a lengthy period for optimal development of an elite-level swimmer. They then hurry home and eagerly try to apply those plans over a period of perhaps 12 weeks (and fewer than 50 workouts) to a group of distinctly average swimmers.

My shift to a teaching emphasis has made me realize that a training emphasis requires more time than a 12-week season (with two and sometimes three meets per week) affords. It has proven to me that the surest way to succeed in short-season swimming — whether high school or summer league — is through emphasis on technique and teaching. Though this seems counter-intuitive to most coaches, I can't help asking, "How can it be a bad thing to move through the water with less effort — no matter the level of the swimmer?"

I've also observed enormous benefits from learning how to make practice challenging every day, not the one-dimensional challenge based on how hard, but a multi-dimensional challenge in which the swimmer is perpetually challenged to combine stroke rate and stroke length to solve the puzzle of how to swim more economically and reduce wasted effort. The yardage total is greater on some days, less on others, but our emphasis has shifted from how many yards to how-close-to-perfect they are.

The Circumstances of this Book

Eric Hoffer, a renowned author and philosopher, worked as a long-shoreman until he was in his 60's. He was often asked if he found the company he kept to be intellectually stifling. He replied that he found no idea so challenging that his co-workers couldn't grasp and appreciate if it was presented simply. This is a quality I can relate to, because my day job is teaching special education. Any good teacher is constantly finding newer, simpler ways to explain things. Virtually no one makes a living as a high school swim coach, which means we have day jobs that occupy our time between practices. It is my hope that this book will help you use your limited time better by suggesting a simpler and more effective approach to coaching.

Where Terry's book is universal, mine is very specific to my situation. It is essentially a journal, largely written between 4 a.m. and 9 a.m. on Sunday mornings. Somehow, my duties as a teacher, a father, husband, etc., kept interfering with my aspirations of being a literary bon vivant. As a result, much of these other aspects of life are interlaced into the fabric of this book, because for swimmers and coaches, these factors have a huge impact on performance.

I include many incidents from my life not because there is anything extraordinary about my small town existence besides its ordinariness. It just seems to me that this very ordinariness is what gives it a degree of universality that might help readers who are unfamiliar with the concepts. What I have found is that a technique orientation is more about a mind-set than it is about the nuts and bolts. It seems that the more ways I can draw on life experiences, the more it secures concepts in my mind and helps me relate it to what my swimmers are doing in the pool.

Although what follows is a chronological account of one high school season, any team in any length season faces virtually all of the same issues when learning to move through the water more efficiently while simultaneously incorporating conditioning into a program. There are also many issues that arise outside of the pool in the lives of swimmers.

Starfish and Offensive Linemen

Two life experiences outside swimming made me realize the impact a coach-as-teacher can have on kids. The most exciting and gratifying moment I ever experienced in athletics was watching my son Judd in a high school playoff game in Rich Stadium. He was a small (160 lbs.) but slow (inherited from me) offensive lineman. Every week, he lined up against tackles and ends who outweighed him by 50 to 100 pounds and game after game his man never touched the quarterback. When the team needed critical yards, they sent the running back through his hole, because his coaches taught him how to use leverage, much as martial arts masters do. His coaches were masters at taking a group of similarly under-sized and under-talented players to a championship by teaching important fundamentals. I could never thank these men enough for giving Judd a sense of belief in himself based on genuine achievement.

The other incident occurred in January of 1998. Tommy Gardner, our JV lacrosse coach was killed when his truck hit a pothole on a country road and slammed into a tree. I was devastated, because he was my good friend, but so was the entire community, because he had been a friend to so many.

The funeral was an incredibly uplifting experience, though, the church packed with lacrosse players from past and current teams. Tommy's mom, our school nurse who had taught Tommy his love of kids, told the coaches that the kids should do whatever made them more comfortable. One of the most hard-nosed kids brought a guitar and sang a tribute he had written the day before. When the service was over, all the kids formed an arch with their lacrosse sticks for the casket and people to pass under on the way out of the church. I still find that I have to choke back tears when I recall that image.

Tommy was important to so many, because as the JV coach, he was the first guy to teach them the skills they needed to become better players. If he was to list 100 rules for successful coaching, I'm sure 99 of them would have something to do with fun. Tommy was a strict disciplinarian, but I'm sure all the kids he coached have the same memory that I do when they think of him — his great cackling laugh.

To help ease my grief, one of my friends gave me a copy of a parable. It ran roughly like this:

An arrogant young man watched as an old man walked down a beach covered with innumerable starfish stranded by a recent storm. Every time the old man passed a starfish, he picked it up and gently tossed it back into the sea.

The young man mocked his efforts saying, "What difference could you possibly make to all those starfish?"

The old man looked down at the one in his hand and said, "To this one, it makes all the difference in the world." And he gently returned it to the sea.

As I said before, none of us is going to make a living coaching high school swimming. None of our kids will make a living as a professional swimmer, so what gives meaning to our efforts? Tommy is not around to do it, and somebody has to pick up the slack. It seems to me that the more tools I have to teach, the more starfish are going to make it. And, when you think about it, is there anything more important?

Points of Reference

Every year in my global studies class when discussing basic religious beliefs, we talk about agnostics – people who question the existence of a god. As a followup, I always give them the following extra credit question:

Question: What does an insomniac, dyslexic, agnostic do at night?

Answer: Stays awake and wonders if there's really a *dog* out there.

There has been an ongoing debate in the swimming community about the benefits of various levels of training volume and aerobic development. I have come up with the definitive answer – just kidding. I do think, though, that we need to take a look at this debate from differing points of view. I sometimes think like the insomniac, agnostic, dyslexic – we're closely studying the problem but are so caught up in our preconceived ideas that we may be missing the vital points.

The historian James Burke tells the story about a philosopher who was listening to a learned man talking about how ignorant medieval men were in the days before Copernicus. He asked, "How could they possibly have thought when they looked at the sun that it traveled around the earth? Any yahoo would understand that the earth goes around the sun."

In way of reply the philosopher simply asked, "And what would it look like if the sun revolved around the earth?"

We see things in a manner consistent with our preexisting perceptions and biases based on our experiences. We enter the yahoo category when we refuse to recognize proof that our view is erroneous or that views that contrast our own can contain some validity.

The Question

If a well-trained and tremendously talented world class swimmer did many laps of naturally perfect swimming while building aerobic base, would it look any different than if that same swimmer covered many laps of naturally perfect swimming while perfecting technique?

Take a swimmer, a Popov clone, a world-class male sprinter who will be in the 6'6" range. Put a very good female high school swimmer who has not been in the water for nine months into the pool next to him. Tell the male that he is to swim a set of 10 x 50 yard swims on 1:00 at 26 seconds holding no more than 8 strokes/length. Tell the 5'2" high school girl just to keep up with the clone.

If asked which swimmer is getting the better practice, most observers would draw the conclusion that it is obviously the girl, as she is probably going to taking at least twice as many strokes to keep up, will look like she is working harder, and will obviously be redder of face and breathing substantially harder as the set progresses, while male swimmer will *appear* to be making no effort at all. Another might say that it is obviously the male swimmer, because he is working on developing his neuromuscular system and practicing skills that will allow him to maintain an efficient stroke at higher speeds, and that while there is little apparent effort, he is making tremendous mental effort to make each stroke as efficient as possible.

In order to truly evaluate the value of this or any training session, it is essential to know the answers to a series of questions. Where in the season is this practice? What did the swimmer do in practice the day, week, or month before? How experienced is the swimmer? How physically mature is the swimmer? What was the specific intent of the set? Then and only then would an observer be able to make a reasonable judgment as to which swimmer got the better workout.

It might be helpful to the reader to know where my biases on some of the basics of a season lie.

Survival of the Fittest

I recently read an article about how man's efforts to eradicate species regarded as pests have influenced natural selection in unintended and unwelcome ways. For example, doctors have widely prescribed antibiotics for infections. These have killed the vast majority of target agents, but those that were immune to antibiotics have survived to reproduce, unwittingly creating far more dangerous, antibiotic-resistant strains of bacteria.

Coyotes were rarely found east of the Mississippi river in the 1800's. When ranchers began to raise livestock in the West, coyotes were hunted, poisoned, and trapped relentlessly. The unintended result was that those animals wily and hardy enough to avoid extermination became progenitors of a super species capable of living in virtually any environment within a range that now extends across the entire continental U.S. and even in urban areas.

Although man has inadvertently contributed to the development of super species, I sometimes think that our benignly motivated attempts to produce a few super swimmers has yielded much the same result. I see the way many coaches, myself included, went about business in the past as being analogous. When the more-and-harder mentality reigned, we could always point to the one or two great swimmers who blossomed and say, "See what a great job we are doing?" Somebody else might look at the majority of the swimmers who did not blossom or quit and wonder whether that was really success.

As we all know, many great swimmers have come out of high-yardage programs. The very best age-group coaches I knew had high-yardage programs. A swimmer I coached in this paradigm holds our oldest school record, in the 500 free.

However, questions remain to be answered.

Are swimmers' accomplishments a product of high-yardage training or of natural selection, which weeds out the lesser athletes due to the volume of less-than-perfect repetitions? It is possible that the naturally great athletes have the kinesthetic awareness to adjust their stroke to avoid using an aching joint and survive to practice another day whereas a less natural talent will continue to use the same stroke until she suffers a disabling injury.

USA Swimming conducted a study that showed that fewer than 10 percent of the swimmers who appear in the Top 16 lists at age 10 are still there at age 15-16. Fewer than 50% of those in the 15-16 rankings also appeared in the 17-18 rankings. I don't find these results to be at all surprising. My experience as an age group coach is that kids who are "world beaters" in childhood or early adolescence are seldom great in maturity. These kids were able to parlay greater size or strength into success in practice and in meets, but often they have inferior technique. Such early-maturing kids tend to be resistant to technique changes, because we all cling to what brought us success previously. As their peers mature, those with superior technique narrow the gap and often surpass their more naturally-gifted peers.

These findings would reconfirm what was for years conventional wisdom – that female swimmers peaked in their mid teens. Once women began to physically mature, few of them were able to progress with heavy training as the main emphasis. Dara Torres and Jenny Thompson are among an increasing number of successful women who have laid this stereotype to rest. Both undeniably came from extensive training backgrounds but revived their careers in their 20's while swimming in technique-based programs.

The Written Practice as Script

One thing that was very difficult for me to accept in adapting a technique orientation is that it necessitates a significant attitude adjustment concerning the sanctity of a posted workout. I used to regularly tell the swimmers who questioned why we were doing particular things in a workout that I really had little to do with creating them, for lo and behold, on that particular morning on my way to school at the intersection of Transit and 20A, a burning bush appeared in the middle of the road. I would stop my car and the voice of God would tell me exactly what she wanted done. I certainly didn't want to make her any madder than she already was with me, so we were going to do whatever she wanted the way she wanted.

When training of energy systems is paramount, it makes good sense to hold to rigidly structured intervals and focus on making them. It makes much good sense to keep intervals and distances consistent when doing benchmark sets. When training the neuromuscular system as well as the cardiovascular, there is going to be a lot of trial and error involved, and the coach must have confidence in his swimmers to provide feedback on how objectives of a particular set could be better met by adjusting distance, repeat numbers, or rest.

The practices presented here are those I feel are appropriate for the high school girls I have coached. Although there is a tremendous gap between the fastest and the slowest swimmer, all of the girls on the team have at least some swimming ability. We have our own 6 lane pool with access for up to 3 hours each day and 4 on Saturday if I choose. Orchard Park is an affluent suburb of Buffalo, NY and my swimmers' parents tend to be supportive and encouraging. It is not a Utopia, but it is what I consider to be an ideal coaching situation. I would caution any coach using workouts from this book to use them as design samples and custom tailor these ideas to the needs of your swimmers.

I have included entire practices for each week as examples. Some weeks there are isolated sets that we used as possible solutions to problems we were working to solve. Most times, we ended up changing a practice as we progressed. Some we finished and some we added to, but I am not a meticulous record keeper and did not make note of changes. I don't feel there is anything sacrosanct about most of my practices; as I have gotten more experienced and tuned in to the fact that I have so many bright, motivated swimmers, my written practices have become more of a general outline for what we want to accomplish than a script to be religiously adhered to.

Individual Medley Training

Among the reasons I am so fond of the IM and have focused so much on it in training is that it is a great life metaphor. I now have all of my swimmers train IM, and have all of my young swimmers focus on becoming good at medley swimming.

I never had any intention of becoming a teacher. On the road to becoming a teacher I have been a stock boy, caddy, lifeguard, steelworker, tire recapper, tree trimmer, roofer, house painter, blacktopper, carpenter, and beer deliveryman. As a teacher, I have taught social studies, math, English, and earth science. For recreation, I windsurf, roller blade, mountain climb, play golf, and road and mountain bike. As a parent of four kids, I have been involved in scouts and coached soccer and baseball. My experience has been that few people have a singular vision of what it is they want to be in life and most try a number of paths; even after selecting a vocation, we all fill numerous roles outside our work.

One of the beauties of the IM is that one does not have to be great in any one stroke in order to become quite accomplished as an IMer. Like so many things in life, one can realize great success in the IM by focusing on a weakness and turning it into a strength.

I used to think that specificity of training was the essence of a successful season plan. If a swimmer was to swim well in backstroke or breaststroke in a short season, there was little time to do anything but train in those strokes. While I agree that the major emphasis should be in a swimmer's best stroke, I have found there is much unexpected value from learning different ways to move through the water efficiently. I also have found that there is a great deal of carryover from one stroke to another; for example, when the hands are in the catch position for breast, it is the same position for a good catch in fly or free.

I also like IM training, because it increases the opportunity for variety in practices and is ideal for warmup, as it works a wide variety of joints, muscles, and tendons without stress. It is great in early season for the same reason. However, as with drill practice, a heavy diet of IM practice allows for much less yardage than a traditional freestyle-heavy training program.

In past years, only a few of my swimmers, those with the most talent, were IMers. Most of my less talented or less experienced kids became sprint freestylers. After I became convinced that virtually all swimmers could be taught short axis skills, we made the decision that all swimmers should be able to swim a legal IM, and would practice all, or at least components of all, four strokes every day. The expected benefit was that we had more kids who could compete for us in the IM. An unexpected benefit was having most of our kids discover talents they never knew they had; many ended up being great in a stroke they had never considered a primary stroke.

Drilling

In sports, there a number of levels of consciousness that go along with the challenge skills continuum of flow in sports. The first level is unconscious incompetence in which the athlete doesn't have a clue as to what she is doing and therefore can't do what the coach is asking. The next level is conscious incompetence in which the athlete is aware of what she should be doing but is unable to for various reasons. The third level is unconscious competence. This is where the body and mind are so well attuned to the activity the body is to perform that the body goes on autopilot and does what is required of it with very little conscious thought.

One of the hallmarks of the great teachers I have had the opportunity to learn from is that though they have a wealth of knowledge, they also recognize that it's not about what they know. What's paramount is a clear understanding of what their students know. Great swimming is less about what is in the coach's mind than what is in the swimmer's, and even more important is what the swimmers know "in their bones."

No matter how brilliantly a concept is illuminated by a coach, there is no substitute for drills that allow the body to directly experience those concepts. My previous resistance to using drills was my long-held beliefs that for every drill, there is a negative aspect of stroke that is being practiced at the same time. An example would be drilling hand lead kicking with the face in the water and then rolling to the sweet spot for breath.

Obviously, no accomplished swimmer is ever going to roll that far to breathe while swimming whole stroke. But by actually using drills with my swimmers on a regular basis, I've realized that "over-correction" of this sort is needed to break their "human swimming" habits.

Swimdown

After every hard set or in preparation for a particularly challenging set, I, like many coaches, told my kids, "Do a 200 (100, 300, 2 minute, 5 minute) swim down." Sometimes in piques of creativity, I would tell them to "do some drills" and watch as kids floated, walked, pulled on lane lines, made plans for the weekend, etc., but rarely did anything that looked like technically great swimming. They knew that if they worked hard on a set, as they virtually always did that I wouldn't get in their face during a swim down.

As my wife likes to say, this can't be rocket science if I am doing it, and after only about 15 years I came to realize what a huge number of opportunities for stroke improvement I missed each season by not structuring this time. By simply substituting specific drills, sensory swims, or drill/swim combinations, we have transformed this wasted time into effective learning time. It is always preferable if the mind is engaged while performing drills, but even if the mind drifts, drilling well forces the body into optimal swimming positions that reinforce proper mechanics at a time when fatigue is a factor. The body becomes programmed to counter instinct and swim with sound mechanics, especially when it is tired.

Calling in my higher math skills, I realized that if we devoted only 6 minutes per day to swim down times 5 practices per week that's 30 minutes each week times twelve weeks is *six hours* over the course of the season of precise practice in what had been previously wasted time.

Learning New Language

One of the issues I perpetually have to deal with is that the kids I work with are by and large vastly more intelligent than I am. Many of them are advanced language students so I impress them with my extensive knowledge of Spanish. *"Juevos verde y jamon"* is Spanish for green eggs and ham. They are duly impressed when I tell them that this is a translation of the title of the book we are doing in my book group and are more impressed to find out that I have gotten to the part about why he does not like them on a train. I am betting my paycheck that the next thing will be why he does not like them on a plane.

A technique-based orientation and its attendant emphasis on drilling forces coaches to expand our vocabularies to include some two-word phrases in a language that is foreign to us – "slow down," "relax more," and "go easier." The advanced versions of these include multi-word phrases like "swim with ease and comfort." After years of exhorting our swimmers to go faster and harder, this is not exactly intuitive, and may require practice in front of a mirror to actually get the words out.

Dryland

Our primary forms of dryland training are stretching and yoga, which we do outside the pool area. Dryland training is a fairly low priority for us because of limited time, but I'd give it more serious consideration in a longer season, or if some of my year-round swimmers wanted to continue a strength program from the summer.

Equipment

We are decidedly low-tech. The most used training tools are Fistgloves and "pdf" fins. The fist gloves are black latex mitts that fit tightly over the hand clenched into a fist. They were invented by Aikido master Scott Lemley to provide increased awareness and sensitivity in the hands by cutting off contact with the water. The swimmer must figure out how to negotiate through the water with minimal help from their hands, and when the gloves are removed, the kids tell me their hands feel gigantic. The immediately better core body balance due to the lack of hand support is an added benefit.

We use small pdf fins mainly for practicing Short Axis drills, particularly body-dolphins. The fins greatly improve these skills, and have been especially valuable for male swimmers. The key is to stress that they should kick as little as possible. I like the smaller rounded ones because swimmers can kick IM's including breaststroke.

We use paddles on a very limited basis, primarily to reinforce the concept of getting the forearms vertical in the water to better anchor.

Season Planning

Bobby Bowden, the tremendously successful football coach of the Florida State Seminoles was asked about specific techniques in defending against the long pass. He commented, "First, you have to back up a lot."

My advice on a season plan is similarly simple – "Slow 'em down and then speed 'em up." Like defending against a long bomb, the start of the season involves a lot of backing up. In our case, it is backing up to fundamentals of streamlining, starts, turns, and basic balance for *all* swimmers. Even the very best can benefit from a review of these critical skills even if it serves mainly as a reminder to those who are already proficient at these skills that they are still to be constantly refined and should always be focal points in a successful practice.

Last year, I had the opportunity of a lifetime to go to Singapore, where my wife's sister and brother-in-law were living. I had the unique experience of participating in a peculiar form of running called a Hash Run. Hashing was invented by Brit's stuck with nothing to do in the jungle, so it, of course, contains a rigorous set of pseudo standards of etiquette and general decorum. It was much like the traditional rugby parties I had attended over the years with the same post-competition beverages.

The idea is that two runners lay out a trail marked with wet flour, in this case partially through the jungle and partially through the streets, and the entire pack of runners collectively begins at the starting signal. The art of laying out a trail is in providing false clues and dead ends for the pack to follow, and having the entire group finish the run in one hour plus or minus

10 minutes. If this does not happen, the people who laid out the trail have to wear a toilet seat around their necks at the post-race gathering.

The genius is that this is not a race – in fact, there are penalties involved for even mentioning the word race. It is a genuine group effort.

The fast guys (FRB's – front running bastards, in hashing terminology) go out ahead of the rest of the pack and they are the ones who find the false trails and dead ends and let the rest of the pack know. If they remain on the trail, they yell "on, on" to the rest of the group so they know to follow.

The entire group virtually always finishes within 10 minutes of the FRB's. The genius of this is that every runner is challenged to run at a level that challenges them, with the better runners going farther and faster. Needless to say, I was not one of the FRB's, and spent most of the run with a guy named Snake Eater who had *twice* jumped out of airplanes and hit the ground before his chute opened.

To me, it is important to focus on creating an atmosphere similar to the Hash Run. For the first few weeks, all swimmers should be swimming at paces similar to those used in a long run. With rare exceptions, the atmosphere should be non-competitive and fun, freeing swimmers to focus on relaxed, smooth swimming. Our first three or four weeks consist primarily of lower-level aerobic work with an emphasis on silent, splash-free swimming.

Speed work is essential from day one, but at the start of the season it is mostly limited to starts, breakouts, turns, half lengths, and widths where the swimmers are taking just a few cycles at high speed. If you commit to slow, thoughtful swimming in practice, be prepared for slow, thoughtful swimming in early meets until the kids find a good match of stroke length and stroke rate that works for them. If time were not a consideration, I would recommend that no swimmers go fast until they have mastered slow speed excellent swimming. Unfortunately, with only 40 or so practices, I always have to make a judgment call for when to add some speed work that isn't necessarily the quality of movement we want to see. Slow, thoughtful, deliberate, focused swimming should be a part of *every* practice.

Intervals

Extended slow-speed swimming could become boring to teenagers, but we keep them engaged by being creative with intervals. I think in terms of intensity and duration instead of distance. We sometimes do repeats where the instructions are to go 5 seconds apart and leave when the 3rd or 4th swimmer touches rather than on a clock interval. On some sets, we stop the rest of the swimmers when the first group finishes a pre-scribed number of repeats. I have included interval times in some of the practices. These should be used as a loose guideline – they were what I felt was an appropriate interval for my swimmers on that given day, and sometimes these intervals were adjusted during the course of practice, usually to allow *more* rest.

Doing Doubles

Some years ago, I attended a conference where Ernie Maglischo, a man I have always admired for his great contributions to our sport, reported that he had tried one-a-day workouts with his Division I colle-giate swimmers and found little perceptible difference in performance compared to when they did double workouts. He did, however, say that his swimmers would again be doing morning practices the next season. His rationale reinforces the concept that great coaches have complex motivations for what they do. Maglischo's reasoning was that he felt that without the prospect of early morning practice, his swimmers would be more tempted to stay up later and engage in behaviors that might not be conducive to great swimming.

Does this mean that there is no reason to do double practices other than to get swimmers in bed earlier? Again, it is a matter of our point of reference.

Maglischo is working with Division I athletes. Although he is highly attentive to technique, he does not have the same daunting task a club or high school coach faces in teaching technique, because his group must have a high degree of natural ability and technical proficiency to rise to that elite level. He would probably have a more difficult time making stroke changes in many of these swimmers though, because most have spent years perfecting bad habits as well as the good ones.

We don't do double sessions once school starts for a very practical reason. Students are not allowed in the building until 6:30 a.m., and homeroom starts at 7:15. It seems to me that results of single-session workouts vs. doubles would be significantly different during a high school season. Maglishco's group of elites is already swimming very, very fast, and the increments of improvement are going to be much smaller than for a maturing, relatively unskilled group. In most programs, double workouts simply allow for more conditioning. If I were to conduct doubles, the primary benefit would be increased opportunities to *practice* and imprint skilled movements.

The belief that is central to this book is that teaching technique is the most important aspect of each and every practice. This should not be misconstrued to mean that aerobic development and challenging sets are not an integral and essential part of our program. They are, but they are given secondary consideration to technique development.

There is no question that, in its initial stages, a technique-based program will be of significantly lower yardage than a traditional training program. On the flip side, if a swimmer demonstrates the ability to practice efficient swimming movements for longer periods of time, there is no reason not to let her do more yardage. A good technique-based program is neither a low-yardage nor a high-yardage program. It is simply a program of committed practice of fluent, efficient movement at whatever speeds or distances the swimmers are capable of. Conditioning *happens*, but it's never the first or only consideration.

What is the Most Important Stroke in a Race?

"7 x 200 on 3:00 – Think about stroke!"

This was an actual part of a workout posted in one of the pools where we practice by a coach who is an adamant critic of Total Immersion, even though he's never read the book, watched a practice, or attended a workshop. The 7 x 200 was standard fare for the workouts posted on the blackboard of that pool. What startled me was that I had never seen anything but times and intervals before, and there was actually a mention of thought.

There weren't any specifics about what or how to swim or what to think, but it seems to me there is a sort of implication that thought may be somehow beneficial to the swimming process. My experience has been that without specific focal points, most swimmers will do a great deal of thinking on a set like this – about Homecoming, weekend plans, or homework, but very little about stroke. Without a specific focus, most swimmers will just "pound out the yardage;" it is my job as a coach to provide focus. It is up to the swimmer to choose or not to choose to focus, but the likelihood of attentive swimming is greatly increased by the inclusion of specific focal points.

As a contrast, Alan Goldberg, a noted sports psychologist who is a regular at the Olympic Training Center wrote, "Too many coaches in this country pound out the yardage at the expense of technique, mechanics, and feel, and in doing so rip their swimmers off. I have been chatting with Olympic swimmers over the past three weeks and so many of them have emphasized how critical the feel is versus just plain dead yardage. Furthermore, when you teach swimmers how to focus on the stroke as a teacher it actually trains them to develop the right focus for racing, and therefore inadvertently helps them handle pressure and swim in their own lane mentally."

My kids would have no trouble answering the question about which stroke is the most important. They would answer as Alan Goldberg would. His answer is that it would be the stroke the swimmer is taking at any particular moment. Any focus on past or future strokes will detract from the one currently being done. It is my goal as coach to have this apply not only to racing, but also to practice as well, and it has been my experience that slow precise drilling and swimming will accomplish this far better than any exhortations on my part.

When I broached the subject for the first time with the kids, I felt we should make it a mantra to never waste one stroke. Immediately one of the kids reminded me that that was not a good goal because it is negative. When asked how it could be made into a positive goal, she immediately replied, "make every stroke count." That sounded good to me.

Einstein and the Golf Balls

Albert Einstein took a golf lesson, and the pro told him about head position, stance, grip, etc. After a while, Einstein called a halt to the lesson, picked up a handful of golf balls, and tossed them to the pro all at once and said, "Catch."

The pro of course missed most of the balls and asked Einstein what the heck he was doing. Einstein replied, "Exactly what you have been doing to me."

No matter how much I try, when I give a set or drill with specific focal points, the kids are usually tuned into it. I have a hard time focusing on that single point. These focal points can be either motion specific (hide your head, show your arm, roll to breathe) or sensory (can you do this more quietly, smoothly, effortlessly). Each can be equally productive. I want to see the whole stroke done the way I envision it. Even after all these years, I have to restrain myself from commenting on more aspects than I should. If I give a set of swims or drills with an emphasis on head position, it is still very hard to focus on that single aspect of the drill and not make comments about hand position, lengthening, etc., etc. It is so much more helpful to swimmers to maintain that singularity of focus to one or two things at a time so that a drill or set doesn't become as meaningless as if there was no intentionality to it. When the swimmer has a limited number of intense focal points, it allows her to sharpen the skill, but also serves to limit input from the self critical conscious mind that says, "I can't do breaststroke," "I am a lousy swimmer," etc., etc.

Taper

To me, the most critical part of taper is infusing a mentality that taper begins on day 1. It is only through diligent and focused effort that the effects of rest will be fully realized. Even though we don't train as hard as as we did in the past.

The only hard and fast rule I adhere to is, when in doubt, rest more.

It is also important to spend considerable time invoking the blessings of the swimming Dog.

WEEK 1
The Journey Begins

"Take almost any path you please, and ten to one it carries you down to a dale, and leaves you there by a pool… There is magic in it."

- Herman Melville, Moby Dick

I went down the path to the dale and the pool, and there was indeed magic there. It is a special kind of magic that those who haven't directly experienced it will be slow to understand.

This is a bonus week for us. We are allowed to start a week earlier than previous years. I made it clear to the kids that it would be strictly voluntary to come to any practices this week and that any conflicts due to work, family obligations, or just plain needing another week of vacation would be no problem. Having lived through the adolescence of three of my own, I understand that voluntary early a.m. wakeups on vacation are welcomed with a zest that is reserved for invitations to activities such as eating ground glass or Vegemite (a taste sensation I recently sampled thanks to my Australian AFS exchange student spending the year with us. I can now understand the key to the Australian athletic success – they feed their kids this stuff and any physical pain or discomfort seems minor in comparison to trying to live with the aftertaste). Yet, on that first day of practice, there were 30 smiling faces anxious to get into the water.

We talked about the upcoming season, and one of the first orders of business was to establish the schedule for the next two weeks before school was to start. I said that I would be glad to come for as long as they wanted to practice. The majority opinion was that we should run double sessions with my proviso that second sessions were strictly optional.

Many friends and cohorts don't understand why I am so obsessed with an activity that the world at large cares so little about, but they have never experienced the exhilaration of a first day with such intrinsically motivated people who are undertaking such an endeavor, forsaking activities that are "fun" and of great importance to peers to embark on a journey that they know will involve a great deal of discipline, as well as physical and mental pain, with no guarantee of success at the end of the road, and embark willingly and enthusiastically nonetheless.

It is my unbiased opinion that no coach will ever work with such a bright, talented, motivated, and fun group of athletes. It is important to the reader to keep this in mind because it is a huge factor in any successes this team achieves.

Walls

Practice for this first week has traditionally focused almost exclusively on drills. I have the luxury this year of having only a few swimmers who do not know these drills, so we will do more actual swimming. We will still be drill intensive as it is essential to instill muscle memory in new swimmers and to awaken latent neural patterns in those who had mastered the drills last season, but who have not done them since. In past years we have spent the first few days with virtually no actual swimming, and it has worked well. It is what I would do again if I were starting with a new group. The emphasis must still be on improving skills by swimming slowly and moving through the drills sequentially. Key drills for the week are:

Long axis (freestyle and backstroke) – balance drills (hand lead and head lead), skating, and switching drills

Short axis (butterfly and breaststroke) – pulsing (hand lead and head lead), stone skipper fly, and SA combo swims

Widths seem to work best for streamlines short axis drilling and dolphining. We will be spending a great deal of time doing widths to perfect breakouts and turns before we do any other drills or swimming. It seems to me that wall work is a traditionally under emphasized aspect of swimming. It is so critical for great swimming at any level, and even more critical in a short season, because leaving the walls is the fastest part of any race and can be as much as 40% of a race if done well. It is critical to maximize propulsion while minimizing drag to carry this speed into swimming. It is important to remember that in a swimming race, the winner is the one who slows down the least.

Focal points for wall work begin with the streamline. I've been teaching it differently after watching Bill Boomer work with a member of the resident team at the US Olympic Training Center in Colorado Springs. I had made the assumption that if a swimmer had reached an elite level, the streamline had been pretty much perfected. I was proven wrong after watching one of the fastest freestylers in the world make noticeable improvements in his streamline after only 10 minutes of Boomer's instruction.

The Core of the Matter

The time I paid attention in my freshman psychology class with Doctor Rotton (real name but no relation to Johnny), he talked about proximal distal development in children. It means that as the child grows, muscles near the core of the body develop before the extremities. This is as it should be in swimming as well. We want to make sure the body core is the focal point of virtually everything we do these first few weeks. This is in stark contrast to what I and many other coaches have done for many years, which was to immediately begin any talk of stroke with a dissertation on the hand, and its entry, insweeps, upsweeps, and outsweeps.

There is the same emphasis in tai chi. In a push, the first movement is from the core and then from the shoulder. I think added emphasis on using the trapezius muscles to get extension on long axis strokes and a second extension on the short axis seems to work on a number of levels. It goes along with more of a core/extremity progression of movements and it seems to help fight the tendency to push down and pull back before reaching full extension. I also think that it creates a longer stroke by focusing on pushing the hands forward with the body vs. pulling the arm forward with the hand.

If you ask virtually any swimmer how to streamline, he will tell you it is done by stretching and reaching the hands as far as they will go. If you watch the side view of a swimmer doing this, invariably the spine will create an arc, which will occupy more space and cause more resistance in the water. We make a subtle shift in focus. Instead of *reaching* with the hands, we try to teach *pushing* the hands forward by contracting the abdominal muscles and trying to move all of the vertebrae *up* while keeping the spine perfectly straight and the head in neutral.

I often tell kids that it's like doing what their moms have always told them not to do – squeezing a tube of toothpaste in the middle. Virtually all of them have heard angry moms tell them to "squeeze the tube from the bottom!"

The key to great breakouts is to practice pushing off into a perfect body position that is as long and thin as possible and then learning to counter instinct and maintain that position as the body slows down. Instinct causes swimmers to fight the water and seek air the quickest way possible by lifting the head. To counter this instinct it is important to have the swimmers focus on maintaining a horizontal alignment and instead of struggling against the water, and patiently wait for the water to gently lift the body to the surface. It seems to work best if the kids focus on having the back of the head, the shoulder blades and the back of the suit all break the surface at the same time. Using the water vs. struggling against it is a key to all great swimming, and this is an easy, dramatic way of introducing this vital concept.

Flow

In evaluating past seasons, it became obvious that a coaching error I committed was that while intensively focusing on the precise development of physical skills, I had not given the mental part of the mind/body connection its due. Lack of mental preparation prevented us from achieving what I felt was the actual potential of a very successful season, and to me, achieving to potential is what it swimming is all about.

I did much reading to improve my knowledge of mental training, and was particularly impressed with Cziksentmihaly's work on a concept he refers to as flow.

In this work he says:

> There is an old Italian adage, *Imparta l'arte, e metitila da parte*, which translated literally means 'learn the art and then put it aside.' It is good advice not only for artists and craftsmen, but also for experiencing flow in sports: Practice the skills to the point you forget you have them. Then abandon yourself to the performance.

> Our beliefs about what we can do are a powerful influence on what we attempt in life. Sport involves the developments of a range of physical and mental skills in the specific sport setting, from maximizing bursts of speed to restraining oneself when the strategy indicates that one should conserve energy. How we perceive our potential to develop these skills in the specific sport settings in which we participate has a profound influence on what we ultimately accomplish and how we feel about it.

Creation of flow is such a beautiful metaphor for what we are working toward in the pool. The emphasis is on creation in that it couldn't be more opposite of "going with the flow" as it is a conscious active process. What we strive for in the early season is precise mastery of skills through a constant and progressively more challenging repetition of specific skills. We need to approach swimming as art and instill a sense of pride in its practice that goes far beyond that which comes from enduring a great deal of pain. We need to relate it to the other arts – music, painting, dance, martial arts, and their like – to get more involved in the process of swimming fast. Swimmers need to learn the mechanics of swimming on such an automatic level that it will require no conscious effort to summon up these skills in competition.

One of the major components of flow in sports is a suitable match between challenges and skills. When challenge exceeds skill level, it produces anxiety. When skills exceed challenges, boredom and apathy result.

Flow is achieved when challenge and skills are both high.

These key elements, skills, and challenges can be developed much more readily in a technique-based approach than in a traditional training program. In a technique based program in which conditioning is emphasized as something that happens while working on technique, the development of skills is continual and the challenges can be multi-dimensional. The challenges can be how few strokes, how silently, how effortlessly, or how fast and how many strokes.

When training with conditioning is emphasized as something that happens while working on technique, the development of skills is continual and the challenges can be multi-dimensional. The challenges can be how few strokes, how silently, how effortlessly, or how fast and how many strokes.

Redefining Challenge

It is important for the coach to teach athletes how to change their perception of a challenge rather than focusing on winning as the sole objective.

In dual meets, it is a rare event in which all of the competitors are evenly matched in terms of ability level. There is little motivation for the swimmer who is markedly slower than the rest of the field or the one who knows she can easily win. Good coaching provides challenges for each of these swimmers by providing specific focal points to work on during the race rather than focusing on winning or other outcomes. These focal points may include stroke count, pacing, wall work, etc.

In the early season, it is critical to give specific, objective, detailed feedback, but as the season progresses, I tend to give progressively less feedback so that by championship time the swimmers can just get up and swim, and "put it aside" and just let the swim happen without thinking about any of the component skills.

The Quest for Balance

This week, our main challenge will be finding balance, or in most cases, rediscovering balance and comfort in the water. This still requires extreme patience. This is an excerpt from the journal I kept during the first season we committed to technique.

> *More kids are telling me they're not feeling balanced this week. Initially I was thinking, "what's wrong with these kids? After all the work we've done on balance, how can they possibly not get it?"*

Suddenly the heel of my palm inadvertently slammed into it's accustomed spot in the middle of my forehead (there's not only a whole lot of forehead there, but there's getting to be an indent there). It's a reaction I have way too often as the obvious sinks in.

> *Last week, these same kids didn't have a clue as to what it felt like to be unbalanced in the water. Lack of balance in the water doesn't leave the great scars I and every other guy who has raced bicycles have. If it did, all swimmers would definitely be more interested in learning what balance feels like in the water.*

> *The only thing bad balance in the water will do to you is slow you down, and the only reason these kids are complaining they're not balanced is that they have experienced perfect balance in the water and know how it's supposed to feel. This is really exciting to me because only the select few naturals who could sense it innately knew what it was supposed to feel like. I also wondered, how many coaches anywhere, any time ever had a swimmer ask them about balance?*

---

*"A work of art is finished only when
an artist realizes his intentions."*

-Rembrandt

I recently had the pleasure of seeing an exhibit called "The Unfinished Print" at the National Gallery at the Smithsonian. It was fascinating to see the progression of Rembrandt prints displayed on the walls. Close scrutiny of the prints revealed that with successive printings, Rembrandt had added or deleted portions of preceding prints. Some of the prints were done as mirror images, and some had color added or went from color to monochrome. Some of the prints were distributed as finished products and then later redone and again distributed as finished projects.

I think that good coaching is artistry as much as it is science. It would greatly surprise me if, in spite of his great gifts and devotion to his craft and though he must have felt an immense satisfaction with his creations, Rembrandt felt that any of his works were perfect. I suspect that as soon as Rembrandt was finally finished with a work, he immediately launched himself into another.

I have shared great elation with my swimmers over great times achieved, meets and championships won, and yet it is my hope that, just as with the great artists, it is the process that is most important.

A Nod to the Gods

In the movie *Tin Cup*, the gifted but erratic pro gives a lesson on the golf swing. While delivering a monologue about all of the elements of the swing, he describes the slight pause at the top of the back swing as a "nod to the gods" because perfection is unattainable. I am convinced that the swim stroke needs its own nod to the gods. Its perfection is unattainable, just as the golf swing should always be a work in progress. *Excellence*, however, is attainable and is a necessary and worthwhile goal. It is vital for both coach and swimmer to understand that in this light any mention of imperfection is just a marker on the road to excellence.

I never want any of my swimmers to feel that they had the perfect swim unless it is their last one ever. Toward this end, it is important to create an atmosphere at this point in the season where no swimmer feels compelled to swim hard in practice. Therefore, the flow rule is in effect. Everything must exhibit qualities of flow – starts and turns as well as swimming. The pool must become a splash-free zone.

It is also critical to establish an environment where kids feel free to experiment in order to find the right combinations of balance, changing rhythm, length, and power that will work for them. This will happen for most by starting at very slow speeds and progressively increasing speed as the qualities of motion and conditioning improve. At this point in the season, we do very few repeats with the clock. Most of the time, we leave at 5 or 10 second intervals and leave when the third, fourth, or last person touches. We also do a great number of widths and spend time on starts and turns.

The New Strokeless Swim (AP)

A Russian security official tied his arms and legs to swim "dolphin style" for 1.2 miles in hopes of persuading the Guinness Book of Records to add a new competition category.

Genri Kuprashvili, 54, undulating like a fish, covered the distance in a swimming pool in 92 minutes and 38 seconds Sunday. Journalists were invited to witness the event. Kuprashvili, who is chief spokesman for the country's security service, hoped his feat would be recognized.

"Such a way of swimming was known in ancient Georgia and was called dolphin style," Kuprashvili said afterward. "In August, I am planning to swim across the Dardanelles Strait, between Asiatic and European Turkey."

Kuprashvili hasn't heard yet whether he will receive official recognition and join Georgia's other three record holders: Dzhumber Lezhava, who did over 3,000 push-ups; Georgy Makharadze, who covered 12.5 miles juggling a ball with his feet; and Dmitri Kiknadze, who lifted 11.3-pound weights tied to his ears.

Once again, there is nothing new under the sun. What I had thought was cutting edge was practiced in ancient Georgia. We still call it dolphining and it is far easier than juggling a ball with your feet or lifting even 10-pound weights with your ears.

Normally, we move from doing wall work to working on long axis drills, but this year we thought we would make the transition from underwater dolphining off the walls to applying it to short axis drills. In addition, again, most of the kids have done all of the drills before.

This most critical movement in the short axis strokes is what Terry Laughlin calls pulsing. My experience is that most people will need to spend lots of time drilling to accomplish this motion with ease and fluency, and that girls will inevitably be able to learn this much quicker than guys.

Emmitt Hines, author of *Fitness Swimming*, describes it as follows:

> I've had a certain amount of success in getting the SA pulsing concepts across by explaining that a persons length and the pulsing rate (rhythm) he chooses pre-determine a waveform of specific amplitude and wavelength that must be followed if the swimmer is to 1) maximize distance traveled with each pulse 2) minimize resistance 3) minimize energy expended. Ever watch a snake slither? The snake describes a 'standing' wave form and glides through that waveform. Each inch of the body goes through the same space – or slides over the same spots – as each preceding inch. In the water this translates to mean the head will break and "roll through" the surface at point A and the shoulder blades will roll through the surface at point A and the butt will roll through the surface at point A then the head will break and roll through the surface at point B and the shoulder blades will roll through point B and... etc. At a moderate pace the distance between Point A and point B should be 80% or more of the swimmers height – so a 6 ft tall swimmer ought to be able to travel 5 ft or more with each pulse or about 12 pulses per length or fewer with arms at his sides. Flippers should only take off about 1 pulse from the count.

Tool Time

According to instinctive swimming, the faster the arms crank, the faster the body will move. I tell the kids that this is like trying to make a car go fast by getting out and spinning the tires by hand. It will work, but it's a lot easier to use the gas pedal and let the engine and transmission do the work. We always stress using the body core as a motor in swimming, because it gives kids a gross motor skill that they can focus on when they race so that they can "swim in their own lane" and not be distracted by focusing on winning, losing, or what the person in the other lane is doing. This works well with the girls, but a lot of guys would consider the tire spinning thing to be cool, because they have that very special stupidity born of testosterone.

This brings up an interesting point for those of you who coach guys. I have done both for many years and find that girls by and large are much more receptive to anything that is process-oriented. If things are explained well, girls will generally buy into a technique-based approach and practice form religiously. Guys want to get a number up there and a lot of times, and need more of a sell job.

Two adages come to mind: 1) to the man whose only tool is a hammer, every problem is a nail, and 2) don't force things, get a bigger hammer. These need to be tempered. Technique sometimes is like adding to the toolbox the equivalent of a *power tool* like a sawzall – an *ultimate* guy tool – that will cut through anything easily when pounding gets old.

Our focus now is on how fast we can move from one side of the body to the other or front to back while keeping everything, especially breathing strokes, smooth. The body will generate any acceleration. This means that in order to go faster on the long axis strokes, it is necessary to move from one hip to the other as quickly and powerfully as possible rather than wind milling the arms, as intuition would dictate. On the short axis strokes it's a matter of sliding forward at a higher rate. It's another one of those things that is so counter intuitive.

Those coaches who are of the "we're here to put the big hurt on 'em, the kids will find their own best way to swim" persuasion will be waiting a long time for body driven strokes to happen for 99% of the kids, especially the guys. I have found most boys are not very successful with body dolphining, because they tend to force things and they also tend not to be very flexible. To counter this, we use fins on virtually all pulsing with the admonition to avoid kicking, and that seems to solve the problem.

The speed generated by some of the weaker swimmers dolphining off the walls was awesome and definitely worthy of the name. I was going to tell them they could be doubles in the next Free Willy movie (I think they're going to have him on a really big ship that hits an iceberg and sinks) but they sometimes don't recognize a compliment. It just worked somehow. When we worked into full breakouts I couldn't believe that all 32 kids got it. Again, if you coach guys, don't be at all surprised if there isn't one who does get it on the first or even third or fourth session unless they are wearing fins.

In addition to the obvious benefits to backstrokers and flyers, I think there are benefits to all swimmers at this stage because of the variety of balance challenges a combination of short axis (fly and breast) and Long Axis (free and back) will provide. (I always tell the kids that there would be no reason to limit distance traveled underwater if there was no advantage to be gained.) I also think that we should experiment with all swimmers (except breaststrokers) using some degree of dolphining off the wall during races. Unless they show that they absolutely can't do it, it seems to me most swimmers will benefit from additional distance off the walls at a higher velocity with less effort.

Peer models are the most effective way that I have found to teach these movements. Have other swimmers put on goggles and watch what is being demonstrated under the water. Quite surprisingly, the best demos for some of the drills are not necessarily by the best swimmers. It is important to look at some of the weaker swimmers during drills with an eye toward using them to demonstrate aspects of a movement. It makes them feel valued and appreciated for providing a real service to the team, and it also inadvertently puts pressure on them to perform, which is good practice for competition.

We had some swimmers walk and then run across the shallow end and timed them. We talked a bit about the difference between running and walking in the water (huge increase in effort, not much increase in speed), and how some of the kids discovered they could go faster by simply turning sideways in the water so that the resistance was halved. They also told me it wouldn't matter if I did it, because I have the same profile front and side. Nevertheless, they had learned the lesson that traveling through the water with less resistance will outdo any gains made by generating more power.

"Women go crazy for a sharp dressed man"

-ZZ Top

One of the things I learned early on living with four women and coaching a female team is that they pay far more attention to my wardrobe than I do. I get daily reminders of what particular elements of my attire are hideously mismatched. I do also, on occasion, receive high praise when the planets are in the right alignment and fortune favors me with a random choice of sartorial splendor that actually matches. This week, I was able to use my woeful fashion sense to my advantage.

Courtesy of my longstanding relationship with my warped friend Jim who used to play with me in Open All Nite, the most oft fired band in the history of music, birthdays and holidays have yielded a closet full of shirts that constitute a museum quality exhibit of tastelessness. (It is not a one-sided exchange. Jim has a gallery of velvet Elvises and an Elvis phone with the Elvis puppet with guitar and mike that gyrates as the phone rings to the tune of "Jailhouse Rock". His wife loves this).

To help set the mood on day one, I wore a standard issue hideously colored shirt with lizards on it and sported a few days stubble. When I got the abuse that I had anticipated from my crew of fashion police, I told them that this was a vacation shirt and I wore it because this was my vacation, and coming to the pool is something I look forward to. I encouraged all of them to take advantage of the open door policy – come in of your own free will and enjoy it – or leave. This part of the year is strictly voluntary, and smiling faces are more important than red ones gasping for breath.

I sported my "Polka or Die" T-shirt one day to bring home the point that what we were about was much more like dance than racing. You don't dance to get to the other side of the dance floor, and at this point in the season, nothing should be about getting to the other side of the pool in a hurry. Some of the girls wanted to adopt it as a team mantra.

I recently read that the new low flush toilets are creating more and more headaches because they need repair so often. The problem is that they need to be flushed numerous times to accomplish what used to be a one-flush operation and ended up using more water. We want to do the figurative "big flush" with the essentials of the mechanics for starts, turns, finishes, and strokes so that we can just provide only gentle reminders as the season progresses, and all of our repairs will be minor.

In honor of this, I wore my maroon with gold trim bowling shirt that has a poker hand with a royal flush in spades on the back that says "Ace High Plumbing, Home of the Royal Flush."

The 200 Fly Made Easy

I did something at practice on Friday that I never thought I would do unless somebody had thoroughly provoked me – I made two of my swimmers swim a non-stop 200 fly. I was watching Martha and Alaina swimming 25's of fly, and they looked so easy, fluid and effortless that I was inspired to challenge them.

Ten minutes before the end of practice I pulled them aside and told them I wanted them to do a 200 fly. I got the immediate reaction that I had anticipated – a look of dismay as they were already very tired. I quickly explained the parameters of the challenge.

They were to swim it only as long as they could maintain rhythm and ease. They were to stop if they started splashing or struggling. They were to go separately so they couldn't compete with each other and were not allowed to look at the clock at the start or finish.

As Keats said, "a thing of beauty is a joy forever." I would have liked to frame those swims and hang them on my mantle as they contained all of the elements we had been working on this week – ease, flow, and apparent effortlessness.

Both of them actually got faster as they got closer to the end, and both were breathing easily when they finished.

An added bonus was that both of them told me that when they realized they were tiring, they just relaxed more.

I'll keep wearing those vacation shirts.

In a book I read long ago, the main character, a mercenary of sorts, had a Japanese garden. In between bouts of annihilating evil, he would tend his garden, constantly moving the rocks in the little stream so that they made just the right sound. I was always struck by the image, but didn't fully understand it.

After this week, I am confident that the garden is in and now it's just a matter of playing with the rocks until exactly the right sounds emerge.

PRACTICE OF THE WEEK—WEEK 1

This week, we devoted all of our time to teaching the drills we would use all season and to beginning the process of making great starts and turns a habit – one that would win many races. Also, when we started a more technique-intensive program, we did much more LA in our practices. This year we had more experience and did much more with fly and breast as an experiment. I wouldn't necessarily advise this if you are new to the process.

In order to see what a first week practice for LA would look like, I asked Terry Laughlin to provide a practice he would have used for sprinters in the first week. It was, after all, the experience of watching the ease and precision that the sprinters he coached at West Point exhibited that inspired me to commit to a program of the same sort.

Warmup set (with Fistgloves):

Kick-Swim 8 x 50

Odd 50's: 1st 25 Slide & Glide (3 breaths each side) – 2nd 25 BK swim

Even 50's: 1st 25 Kick in skating position – 2nd 25 FR Swim

Notes: Slide and Glide is simply a more active form of BK kicking, rotating (with a stroke and recovery) from Sweet Spot left to Sweet Spot right. Skating is our favorite way of practicing flutter kicking for freestyle. The focus on this set was on keeping the head aligned with the spine on both kicking and swimming. Doing it in alternate FR and BK repeats points up the similarities in both strokes. On the FR 50's, alternate kicking and breathing side by 50's.

Swim 12 x 50 Swim Golf on 1:00

1-4 FR, 5-8 BK, 9-12 25BK25FR

Long Axis Combo Main Set

Do 4 rounds of 150+100+100 on Rest interval of 3 yoga breaths. Rest 1:00 between rounds.

150 = 50 LA Combo Kick – 50 3-ct Slide & Glide – 50 LA Combo Drill.

100 = LA Combo Swim 4BK3FR.

100 = Swim 25BK25FR25BK25FR. Count strokes and take time.

Descend Golf Score for 100 Swim over 4 rounds.

Notes: LA Combo kick means alternating one cycle of Slide & Glide and one cycle of Skating. LA Combo Drill means one cycle of Slide & Glide alternating with one cycle of Underswitch. The final 100 in each round is done as a Swim Golf exercise (add up total stroke count for 100 yds plus time) with a goal of improving your score on each round. This puts the emphasis on using the first 250 yds (150+100) of each round to improve your sense of slipping a long sleek bodyline through the water.

Swim 2 rounds of: (4 x 50 + 4 x 25)

1st round: 50's = 25 3-ct Slide & Glide + 25 2-ct Slide & Glide; 25's = Underswitch

2nd round: 50's = 25 2-ct Slide & Glide + 25 1-ct Slide & Glide; 25's = Zipperswitch

Kick-Swim 8 rounds of 2 x 25 Odd 25's = BK   Even 25's = FR

Notes: Start with 2 x 25 @ 6spl, and add 1 spl on each round. The final round will be swum at 13spl for both BK and FR. This is really an "active kicking" set as the idea is to kick (strongly but silently) and glide just enough in each stroke cycle to complete 25 yards in the assigned number of strokes, while maintaining an efficient steady kick on every length throughout the set. The amount of glide will be gradually reduced as one stroke is added after each pair of 50's. The action changes gradually from "kicking-with-strokes-mixed-in" to swimming with a smooth, steady kick. This is one of the best ways to teach kicking that is completely integrated with fluent, whole-body propelling movements, which is a far more valuable exercise than any amount of kicking on a board.

Swimdown: 400 Silent 25 LA Combo + 25 BK + 25 LACombo + 25 FR

Wall Work

Because winning the turns is a key aspect to winning the races in a short season, wall skills (turns, pushoffs, breakouts) are the first skills we practice each season. Here are some examples of how we introduced wall skills.

We do these cross-pool, usually doing 4 to 6 reps of each task in 2 heats:

Freestyle Breakouts

- No kick push-off with hands at sides and head lifted and looking forward. When momentum stops, kick easy to other wall.

- Same, but moving head to neutral (look directly down) with no kick from the wall. Focus on keeping balance and break the surface with back of head, shoulder blades, and butt at the same time.

- Same, but with arms tightly streamlined.

- Streamlined push-off on side, with fast narrow kick and roll to stomach. Continue fast kick to the other wall.

- Same, but with one breakout stroke stressing pulling the body *forward* over the hand and keeping the head in line (virtually all swimmers instinctively lift the head up to some degree as they break out.)

The focus of this set is to improve awareness of maximizing breakout speed and distance by progressively moving from body positions with drag and resistance to fast, efficient streamlines. As Fistgloves inventor Scott Lemley says in his Commandments of Swimming, "Find the path of greatest resistance, then find the path of least resistance." Emphasize that, all things being equal, a longer body will travel through water faster. It's also vital to stress that simply moving the head from looking at the bottom to looking forward *doubles* frontal resistance. As the drills progress, each swimmer will *feel* lower resistance and more speed.

Turning skills

The next focus after leaving the walls is on turns. I have found that the best way to teach them is to break them into the smallest component parts.

1. Ball float balance – have partners watch for anything not tucked. Pay attention to chin tuck, so the head is inside the body-ball.

2. Prone balance – pay attention to how arms help balance the rest of the body.

3. Move from prone balance to tight tuck, then back to prone. This mimics the approach, turn, and breakout, on short-axis turns.

4. In shallow end with partner, assume tight tuck and have partner spin by placing an arm under the shins and a hand on the back. This gives the sensation of fast rotation in long-axis turns.

5. Unassisted move from prone balance to front somersault. Work with partner to assure initiation with a chin tuck and no splash.

6. Push off from the wall, on surface, and somersault at the near flags with maximum speed.

7. Swim freestyle. Somersault every 5 strokes (This can be changed to any *odd* number to force the swimmer to initiate the turn with either hand.)

Backstroke turns are simple now. Have the swimmers do long axis combo drills-5 strokes free, 5 back, with a somersault as they transition from free to back to free. This naturally teaches the free-back turn. Teach breast and fly with the same progression only moving from a prone float to somersault backwards.

Basic Drills for Basic Skills

We used the following drills to develop core movement for breaststroke and butterfly swimming as well as using it to rocket off the walls in freestyle and backstroke starts and turns.

Head-Lead Body Dolphin. Float in balance, face down arms at your sides and start a relaxed, rocking body motion by rhythmically pressing your chest into the water. Set up a wave-like action that runs down the body, just as a wave runs through a garden hose when you snap one end of it (or as one my better math students suggested, duplicate a sine wave). Try to make every inch of the body pass – head, torso, hips, knees, feet – through the same space in the water. Breathe every 6 to 8 pulses. Breathe within your body motion and without jutting your chin. Keep knees flexible, but remember that this is a body motion, not a kick. All body dolphins are body driven.

I have found that the most effective way of practicing this is by doing widths underwater. It is important to emphasize a slow *body* motion because most swimmers will have a tendency to over-kick, and to make it a speed contest.

Hand-Lead Body Dolphin. Same drill as above but extend both arms forward with hands at shoulder-width. Focus attention on keeping the hands weightless. Swimmers tend to seek resistance with their hands because it makes them feel like they're doing something positive. Watch for hands that travel up and down with the body creating drag. Emphasize driving the hands *forward*.

Additional Sets of the Week

Working on Rhythm:

LA
- Sets of 4 x 25 with 3, 4, 5, 6, cycle bursts ez kick to wall.

SA
- Sets of 4 x 25 with 7, 6, 5, 4 strokes increasing speed as stroke number drops.

Note: The purpose of these sets is to let swimmers experiment with faster rhythms. It is critical at this point in the season that the coach monitors for splash, struggle, lack of rhythm, and hard breathing. Most kids will have a tendency to go too hard. Remember the concept is easy, relaxed speed. This set is a mainstay of our season. There are many combinations – reversing the order, going from slow to fast or fast to slow, swimming sets of 4 at each stroke number, etc.

Working on Turns:

LA
- 10 x 50 from midpool

- hand-lead side kick, swim backstroke inside the flags and do a turn and breakout with at least 7 dolphins

SA
- 10 x 50

- 25 breast to turn, breakout and double pulldown, EZ kick on back. At this point in the season, the emphasis should be on breaking out as far down the pool as possible

6 x 25 LA Combo with somersault transition.
Swim 4 strokes of backstroke, somersault and do 3 strokes of freestyle. Or 3 of back and 4 of free.

10 x 50 Backstroke, Hand-lead kick

Switch to backstroke swimming from the flags to the turn and practice tight dolphin off walls to breakout.

Working on IM Skills:

LA emphasis

- 125 IM's alternating 50 fast back and 50 fast free. All EZ lengths should be done @ no more than–2 spl

- Odd: 25 Fly EZ, 50 Back **Fast**, 25 Breast EZ, 25 Free EZ

- Even: 25 Fly EZ, 25 Back EZ, 25 Breast EZ, 50 Free **Fast**

SA emphasis

- 150 IM's: 25 Fly **Fast**, 50 Back EZ, 25 Breast **Fast**, 50 Free EZ

- Do the 50 of each LA stroke @-3spl as recovery. All swimmers should wait for the lane to clear for each fast 25 so everyone has the opportunity to swim Fast SA down the middle of the lane.

Practice for Starts (illustrated on video)

- Three hip-ups, mount blocks, dive for height

The emphasis here is on attaining height by focusing on snapping the hips and getting them above the head. The entry should have hands, arms, shoulders , torso, legs and feet going through the same small hole in the water. There should be little splash on the entry.

Relay Start Pickups (4 to 6 cycles)

- Step-up starts and have swimmers on blocks do a wind up relay start and then *jump* for distance

Incoming swimmers:

Finishes

- The incoming relay swimmers go from the midline of the pool and focus on great finishes.

I think our veterans genuinely appreciate the value of great finishes as we lost our first meet in three years because we got touched out in three races by a combined total of 12-one-hundredths of a second.

Focus for finishes should include:

- Finish on your side

- Watch your hand as you drive it into the wall with your body

- Always touch below the surface

Pushoffs—Widths

- 10 Superman (head looking at the wall, arms apart) push-offs, kicking to the other side (I tried to be politically correct and use Superwoman, but the girls told me that Superwoman would not be so stupid as to make so much more work for herself)

- 6 x tight streamline kicks focus on the ease of great streamlining vs. the superman position

Body Dolphin Practice – Emphasis on NOT kicking. Have swimmers watch and critique each other, asking "How is that dolphin-like?" May use small fins selectively with some swimmers.

- Head-lead body dolphin

- Hand-lead body dolphin – Focus on ease and driving hands forward.

Drill/Swim with Fistgloves

4 rounds of 4 x 75 drill and swim. Drills are as follows by rounds: 1)EZ Anchors, 2)Triple Underswitch, 3)Triple Zipperswitch, 4)Triple Overswitch.

1st 75: 50 Drill/25 Swim

2nd 75: 25 Drill/50 Swim

3rd and 4th 75's: Swim with Focus from Drill

10 x Deep Nose Breath

Focus on expelling air by contracting abdominals

Remove Fistgloves

Pick one Focal Point from Drills, EZ Silent Swim for 10 Minutes

Working on Distance Per Stroke:

LA
- 10 X 75

- Do each 75 as: 25 each of 3 count glide, 2-count glide and EZ swim. Swim @–3spl (3 strokes fewer than your usual count for 25 yards.)

SA
- 7 rounds of 3 x 25

- Do each round as 25 each of 3-count-glide breast, 2-count-glide breast, choice of fly or breast.

- For both sets, choose a rest interval that puts no time pressure on the swimmers. One way to do so is to have them rest for a given number of deep, slow (or "yoga") breaths — perhaps 5 breaths. Another is to send them off at 10 second intervals with first swimmer to start next repeat when 3rd swimmer in lane finishes.

Note: Emphasize that all breaststroke swimming must include a fast-hands recovery. On slow breaststroke, keep the long glide between strokes, but the hands should still ***shoot*** forward.

Turn sets:

LA 10 x 50
Kick in Sweet Spot in hand-lead position; swim backstroke inside the flags and do a turn and breakout with at least 7 dolphins.

SA 10 x 50
Swim 25 breast, turn and do double underwater pulldown, then EZ kick on back to starting wall. Emphasis long pushoff on breakouts on both walls.

IM Sets:

LA
125 IM's alternating 50 fast back and 50 fast free. No more than – 2 s/l

SA
150 IM's as follows: 1 x 25 fast fly and breast, with 50 of each LA @–3 as recovery. All swimmers wait after each stroke so that each swimmer has the opportunity to swim SA down the middle of the lane.

WEEK 2
Rhythm but No Blues

We also are including yoga as part of warmup. We are experimenting with a series of exercises called Salutation to the Sun. It is slow, emphasizes balance and core movement, seems to cover a full range of motion, and has an emphasis on controlled breathing. During the year, we will try to do a set number of cycles of the Salutation to get us ready to swim.

During the practice, we did our 3 hip-up start drills then relay starts with a dive. We did about 5 minutes with freestyle pickups and then about 5 minutes with the finishers coming in breaststroke to give them some experience with short axis finishes and to prepare them for the fact that there are many different people who could be together on a relay at various points in the season.

This week, I am also having the more experienced kids pick one drill to focus on. While doing that drill, they are supposed to pay attention to a single aspect of it as they do a continuous swim for 10 or 15 minutes. I think this is highly effective for kids with good mechanics, but feel it would be counterproductive for lesser skilled swimmers, as they would in all likelihood be perfecting bad habits. The newer kids should do these as 25's so that corrections can be made often.

We tried this set a few times, and pulsing drills with fins on seemed to be a highly effective way to influence short-axis body movements. It seems that rather than being boring, these swims seem to have a meditational quality to them.

R & B – If these two letters bring to mind 'Retha Franklin, Wilson Pickett, and Otis Day and the Nights, you're not only old like me, but you're half right. The R is definitely all about rhythm, but ain't no blues here this week. The B is all about breathing. It is our goal to focus on head position that will make it easy to breathe without disrupting the flow of the stroke. This is among the most counterintuitive skills to be learned as instinct tells us to go where the air is-straight up.

We will be working on keeping the rhythm flowing and gradually increasing speeds. Toward this end, it is important for me to remind myself that we need to go easy and effortlessly. There is such a temptation with all this beautiful, balanced, flowing swimming I'm seeing to put the hammer down.

I feel like a guy who drives his new Porsche off the lot and into a rush hour traffic jam. At some point, it will be pedal to the metal, but it's hard to wait.

How Fast Can Arnold Schwarzenegger Swim??

I refer to my four-year-old nephew as Mr. Muscles with the emphasis on the Mister. Our ritual greeting consists of me checking out his bulging biceps that he refers to as his pipes, which must measure an astounding 2 inches when he has them fully pumped. I think he is like any four-year-old who when told to "make a muscle" will automatically flex his bicep.

In practice before we did a set, I asked one of the girls who is a national class rower to "make a muscle." She has such genuinely impressive biceps that we have had an ongoing debate about the appropriate tattoo to adorn them with. She did just as my nephew did and flexed her bicep. So did the 8th grader, the sophomore, the junior and the senior.

My question was, "What does this have to do with swimming?" It was followed by a brief moment of silence and then the response: "We need to use our bodies to swim fast, not our arms." Right on the money.

We followed this up with a set of 10 x 50, which had a dual purpose. The 50's were actually 48's. The instructions were to swim easy on the first

25 and then do a somersault at the T without touching the wall. Then, on the second 25, the swimmer has to build to the fastest rate she can manage.

The no-wall turn is a great way to generate great speed coming over, and there is an added bonus because there is no momentum coming off the wall. The swimmer must accelerate and will be sorely tempted to do what feels most natural – try to generate momentum with the arms. The focus of the set is to get momentum going with the body and generate the buildup from faster core rotation rather than slapping the water, which will inevitably *feel* better and more propulsive.

It is also an important set as it is inevitable that even the best swimmers will at some point blow a turn in competition, and will be better prepared to deal with it with practice experience.

I make it a point to mention the body rhythm every time we do a descending set, and now when I do, the "Polka or Die" chant starts up.

An Insider's View of Breaststroke

Most of the lessons I have learned about *teaching* breaststroke came from my good friend Glenn Mills. Glenn has some interesting ways about him, but he did spend about half of his life in the absence of oxygen while perfecting his pulldowns. When he is lucid, he is more knowledgeable than anybody I know on the workings of the most difficult of strokes, so I asked him to describe what great breaststroke is all about in his own words.

Breaststroke Perspective
From a guy who used to be really good at it

By Glenn Mills

I love swimming breaststroke. I always have. What a cool stroke! The best thing about breaststroke is that timing is everything. When your timing's on – the rhythm, the glide, the smoothness, the power, the ATTACK – there's no other feeling quite like it in the water. Other strokes seem boring by comparison – and way too simple. Breaststroke is *exacting*.

You have to do each part perfectly...and then combine them to create flow. There's also the yin/yang thing. In breaststroke, you have to alternate from a gentle press against the water and a silent glide, to an explosion of energy as you attack into the next silent glide. One second your hands are sensitive, as they feel for the right place to hold on to the water, the next second they're moving so fast you can barely see them, as they shoot forward to set up for the next stroke.

Did I say that the best part about breaststroke is that timing is everything? Well, it's also the *worst* part about breaststroke. There's so much to do right that when one piece falls out of line, the whole thing breaks down. That's when the real search begins – the search to get your timing back, to get your pull just right, to angle your head and neck just right, to grab the water just right with your feet. You have to look at it as a challenge, almost like a hunt. Then the work becomes fun.

The biggest problem for short-season breaststrokers (and their coaches) is that they have limited time to search for the elusive Perfect Timing. The problem gets even bigger if they try to find Perfect Timing while swimming 10 X 200 breaststroke sets on a 3:00 interval. Here's a secret: Many great breaststrokers devote a *major* portion of their practice time to drills. They work tirelessly on the individual parts of their stroke (using drills) and practice whole-stroke breaststroke only in short, focused sets – at or just under race pace.

Many swimmers and coaches, especially those with short seasons, feel that drills are a waste of time, and that they take away from time needed for conditioning. I say: These folks haven't tried the right breaststroke drills! First of all, many breaststroke drills call for the swimmer to breathe on every other stroke cycle. Some call for you to pull or kick or undulate for several stroke cycles – under water. Talk about conditioning! After several weeks of doing nothing but the right breaststroke drills (OK, with maybe some freestyle thrown in because Coach says you have to), normal breaststroke will feel like a piece of aerobic cake. Second, breaststroke drills help you isolate and develop the perfect timing for each aspect of the stroke. When each part is right, it's easier to put the whole stroke together and make it flow.

Timing issues usually come down to swimmers trying to kick or pull TOO BIG. If they pull too far back, it makes for a strong pull, but a slow, resistive recovery that can throw off their whole-stroke timing. If they draw their feet right up to the butt, it creates a huge surge forward, but exposes the thighs to the water and stops the swimmer in his/her tracks. For most swimmers, the urge to kick or pull TOO BIG is instinctive. I've learned this from coaching other breaststrokes and from lots of frustrating personal experience. My instinct as a competitor was to grab the water, hold it, work with it, and feel that I was exerting maximum effort (which I once thought was equal to power) in each stroke. When I got into a race, all I thought about was racing and grabbing as much water as possible. Even when I worked on smaller, quicker, more accurate movements in practice, when I got into a race, my excitement would overcome my mind. As a result, my kick got bigger and my pull got wider. I *felt* like I was trying as hard as I could, but I wasn't getting the result I wanted. All I was doing was creating drag. I knew I had to search harder.

For me, in the old days (mid 1970's and early 80's), the search was done with surgical tubing. I tied one end of it to the wall, tied the other end around my waist, and swam to a point where the tubing started to twang. I positioned myself right next to the lane line and started swimming. The lane line was my reference point. If I stayed even with my marker, that was *good*. If I started to slip backward, even for an instant, it meant there was a dead spot in my stroke and I had to work it out. I did this by adjusting things such as leg angle, ankle and foot position, hand position, the width of my pull. What I discovered was that the better I got at eliminating drag, the less *work* I had to do to stay even with my lane marker. The important thing wasn't how hard I could pull or kick, but how efficient I could be. Less was almost always more.

If you doubt this less-is-more idea, please take a look at tapes of the world's greatest swimmers. They make it look easy. I learned more from watching Tracy Caulkins swim than from any other swimmer. She was a true master – in every stroke and every aspect of swimming and racing. I once watched her win the 400 IM at long-course nationals – by 25 meters. The entire time I was watching her, one thought kept going through my head: 'I wonder how fast she would be if she tried.' Yes, she was born with great "feel" for the water, but what made Tracy truly great was her ability to work, search, invent, and DISCOVER what it was that made her faster and more efficient. She was a professional at her sport. She was pure artistry.

Back to the surgical tubing…I would recommend this kind of thoughtful, tethered swimming to any modern-day breaststroker, but remember that in the 70's and early 80's, your head wasn't allowed to go under water. I could always keep that lane marker in sight. If you do the "wave" breaststroke, you may be too deep to see the lane marker. You could try doing tethered swimming in the shallow end, so that you can use the tiles at the bottom of the pool as your marker, or you could use breaststroke drills.

Some of my favorite breaststroke drills are done under water. Under water there are no distractions, and you can feel the water on all the surfaces of your body. You can also use the tiles on the bottom in the same way I used the lane markers. If you stop moving past the tiles, you have a dead spot in your pull or kick.

One great drill is underwater breaststroke kick, done with your extended arms held in a perfect streamline. Take three or four or more kicks under water, adjusting your angles and width until you can see the tiles whizzing by with no pauses. Another drill is underwater breaststroke pull. Use a dolphin kick (flippers make this even more fun) and take three or four or five or more armstrokes under water, searching for the width and rhythm that feels fluid and fast. And keep watching those tiles. If you're willing to experiment when you do these drills, you will be amazed at how much you can learn about drag and timing, rhythm and stroke rate. You may also find that taking a smaller pull or smaller kick eliminates dead spots. Less may be more.

Experimentation is the key. The best breaststrokes, in my opinion, are those willing to work both on their own and with their coach to experiment on every aspect of their technique and race strategy. They're the ones willing to devote a lot of practice time to drills, and not afraid to try different race strategies in their early meets. Breaststroke is all about discovering Perfect Timing. The smallest dual meet, if you use it for thoughtful, planned experimentation, can prove to be the most important race of the season. Which leads to another issue...if you have a good breaststroker on your team, and you're swimming against a weak team, your swimmer may cruise through his/her race. DON'T LET THEM DO IT. Explain to them that there are going to be times when they have no one to challenge them. That's the time to experiment and to learn to swim because of personal pride and the challenge to become the best swimmer you can possibly be.

I think back to the swimmers from whom I learned the most: Mary T. Meagher, Rowdy Gaines, Craig Beardsley, Tracy Caulkins. All legendary. They outswam...make that DESTROYED...everyone in the country and in the world in their specific events. They couldn't depend on other people to push them; they had to do it on their own.

Demand this type of focus and personal commitment if you're a breaststroker or if you are coaching breaststrokers, even if your season is short. ESPECIALLY if your season is short! Don't be afraid to use drills, but make sure they are done *perfectly* and with great focus, even if that means they are done slowly and not on an interval. And...oh yeah...save time for some REALLY FAST sets. They can be short, and short distances (25's, 50's, and 100's), but make them focused and FAST. This is the time to put all the parts together. Get your aerobic training from that freestyle thing (or from EXACTING breaststroke drills). Use slow sets and drill sets for discovery. Demand feedback. If they don't give you feedback, they're not searching and you might as well put them in the freestyle lane and WORK THEM HARD. There is simply no easy way to become a great breaststroker. If you're not hurting, you'd better be thinking.

Breaststroke is a search. There are countless styles, countless opinions, countless ways to achieve success. The way to find the style that's best for you is to experiment and search. Like I said...no easy way. That's just one more thing that makes breaststroke the coolest stroke.

Stations Workout

I'm very fortunate to have Deb Dourlain as my long time assistant coach. She is a former record holding swimmer and has a great eye for detail. She also has a much better capacity to coach starts than I do, and she is great at picking up fine points when doing analysis of video.

She also coaches our divers when we have them.

A tremendous advantage of a TI approach is that it offers very specific and easily recognizable focal points to use in stroke evaluation.

Sometimes a coach or an assistant might not have a great deal of experience in swimming. This is a disadvantage, but many successful coaches have come from other sports.

Even a neophyte could provide valuable feed back to swimmers who have been taped if given specific instructions in what to look for i.e. head position, body roll, etc. As time progresses, I'm confident most kids will need little help in evaluating tapes of themselves because they will quickly come to recognize the key aspects of great swimming.

On Tuesday we did a stations workout. After warmup, each group stayed in one lane for 12 minutes and then moved to the next lane. Fortunately, my son, who is a very talented coach, was available to take a station. He taped one 50 of choice for kids in his station and then gave them a stroke critique. I have no idea what he told them because I have absolute faith that he understands the principles we are working on, and will probably have a slightly different way of explaining the same thing than I do which I think is a positive.

When I was teaching turns, I came across a good example of the benefits of creating an environment in which it is acceptable to fail. I wanted to try some new ideas I had been kicking around about doing better backstroke turns, having the kids push of the wall on their backs, roll to their stomachs, and then do a fast somersault before reaching the near flags. I could visualize what I wanted, but couldn't quite explain the sequence of how to do it, so I explained it as best I could to the kids and we experimented for a while.

All the swimmers volunteered their ideas. It was rather comical at first because the attempts were very awkward. Everyone laughed about the numerous failures and had a good time as we got closer and closer to what we wanted. It was great to see that they could laugh at themselves and to understand that the laughter of others was at the expense of the situation, not at them as people. Eventually, we settled on a one hand on the side, one hand leading, pull down to the stomach while throwing the side arm to the front somersault. It accomplished what we wanted, which was simulation of a high speed entry into a turn.

"You can achieve your aims through the encouragement of others. Encouragement is one of the great powers. Kindness and gentleness in your relations brings allegiance, cooperation and ultimately success."

-I Ching no. 58

In an effort to improve our mental training, I took a cue from the writings of Keith Bell and others and drafted a statement of excellence with a number of points which will help us to become the team we are capable of being. I don't feel that any of the points are going to be a radical departure from past practices of this team as we have been blessed with excellent people who do most of these things as a matter of course. I take most of the points as a given in practice and have never seen a need to formalize things, but I can't see how doing so would be anything but beneficial. I think the value of this document is that it will make everybody more conscious of their actions and their consequences on others as well as themselves – both positive and negative – and the more conscious we are of our actions, the more likely they are to be repeated or corrected as necessary.

To prepare for this, I created a PowerPoint presentation with illustrations of each of the concepts. We viewed it in my classroom and then had questions and discussions about each of the points so that everybody was clear on exactly what was entailed by signing the document.

Orchard Park Swimming Statement of Excellence

1. I am responsible for making the program work for myself and everyone else on the team.

2. I will accept every team member as a person. I will respect her rights to pursue excellence. This includes myself.

3. I place a high value on the pursuit of excellence. I will keep the pursuit of excellence and victory enjoyable. I will do everything I can to help my teammates to pursue excellence.

4. I will treat practice as an opportunity.

5. I will embrace physical and mental challenge because I know it is necessary to make my team and myself stronger.

6. I will encourage others to embrace challenge and to make challenge fun.

7. I will enjoy swimming and I will express my enjoyment in practice and competitive situations. I will encourage others to talk about the fun.

8. I will thank others on the team for their encouragement and support.

9. I will thank my coach for challenging me to better my physical and mental skills.

10. I will express complaints only to a person who can do something about the problem. When I voice concerns, I will offer solutions for correcting the problem.

11. I will encourage my teammates to remind me when I am not focused, or am acting in a negative manner. I will thank them for reminding me and for taking the responsibility to help my team and me.

12. I have no interest or use for excuses. I don't need to protect myself from others opinions by making excuses before or after I swim.

13. I realize that failure is an important part of success. I will use my failures to make myself stronger.

Signature_____Date_____

It did not take long to realize benefits of the program. I have heard more "thank you's" in practices than ever before. I have never coached in a more positive, relaxed, focused and fun environment.

One of the highlights was when one of our best swimmers pulled me aside at the end of practice to share a story with me. She told me how she had praised one of her teammates who made great progress last year and is now swimming with the best groups in practice. She pointed out how improved her stroke was and how hard she was working.

That afternoon she received a call from the girl she had praised in practice. Her message was that she appreciated the praise she had received and was so encouraged that her progress had been noted by a swimmer she had always looked up to as a role model.

What if all of the world could get caught up in such a positive cycle?

Rosie the Riveter

When I was in DC this summer, my 12-year-old daughter was intrigued by an exhibit that featured Rosie the Riveter. Rosie was part of a PR effort on the part of the government to get women to work in the factories during the war while the men were off fighting. It surprised me that she wanted a poster for her room with a picture of Rosie flexing her impressive bicep with the caption, "WE CAN DO IT !!!"

I mentioned Becca's interest in Rosie to my captains and they decided that they would adopt Rosie for this year's T-shirts. The shirts came in and they make a strong statement. Quaker Swimming 2001 with Rosie and the "WE CAN DO IT" caption.

I can't fathom some of the teams from my earlier years coaching the girls' team wanting anything resembling Rosie on a team shirt. In the past, I was dismayed beyond measure when I would give out hard sets and they would tell me they couldn't do them because "we're only girls."

As the saying goes, "You've come a long way baby." The girls see strength and toughness as qualities that are not at all unfeminine and in fact something to be proud of.

A Dog's Life

I was at a friend's house for a party and was admiring his gorgeous Alaskan Husky. (No, everybody in Buffalo doesn't own one. We sometimes borrow our neighbors' to pull our sleds.) We had owned a Malamute years ago, and as Greg and I compared notes we found that they had very similar tendencies. They are fabulous dogs, beautiful, incredibly intelligent and loyal, but whenever they get loose they have a tendency to help small animals find their way to the great beyond.

Greg lives in a subdivision with fussy neighbors. They take exception when their cats and pet rabbits get eaten, and to accommodate them, Greg invested in an invisible fence.

The principle of the invisible fence is that the dog is equipped with a collar that delivers a shock when he approaches the boundaries of his property. The idea is to make the dog think that the only place he is safe is in his yard.

The dog has a great deal of incentive to stay in the yard. He has people who love him and care for him, and wait on him paw and paw. He has even trained them to give him Milk Bones when he barks. He is in a dog's vision of heaven on earth.

In addition to leading an indulged life, he has learned that if he approaches the edge of his yard, there will be negative consequences.

Unfortunately, Greg's dog has learned a great life lesson. He soon came to realize that the maximum range of the electric field is only about 30 feet. By accident when the temptation of chasing squirrels that were heaping abusive squirrel taunts at him from just the other side of the yard got to be too much for him, he discovered that if he put up with a good jolt for a brief period of time, he could get his freedom. It was not only freedom to chase squirrels, but total freedom to wander the neighborhood and boldly go where no Husky had gone before. In addition, he has also learned that when he comes back, he will be welcomed home, be fed, have his belly rubbed, and continue to get dog snacks.

Because the trip outside of the yard was so rewarding to his dog, Greg tried to increase the intensity of the field to just below vaporizing level. His efforts were to no avail as the dog learned that if he could endure just a bit more pain, he could have his freedom.

It struck me how similar the great coaches I know are like Greg's dog.

We all have a tendency to get into comfort zones – physically, mentally and emotionally – that are restricted by real or perceived barriers. We tend to stay there because it is comfortable for us, and we know if we venture too far out, there are inevitably going to be some negative consequences.

The great coaches are always looking for new ways to motivate, condition, or improve technique in their swimmers. They don't embrace change simply for the sake of change, and are not afraid of failure because they know they can always return to what they have done before.

The biggest difference between our situation and Greg's dog's is that we choose whether we wear the collar or not.

The Visit

One of the highlights of the week took place when Jim White, a coach from downstate brought his team to practice. Jim's team is in Johnson City, which is about a 3½ hour drive from here. He brought his team up on a bus to do some technique work with us and then go to an amusement park nearby.

This is impressive on a number of levels. The fact that he would arrange this on his own time speaks volumes about his dedication to his kids. In addition, Jim is coordinating a "Swimmers Against Drugs and Violence" invitational meet in which all participants must write an essay stating how swimming has helped them to avoid drugs and violence.

Jim is a successful veteran coach who is still seeking new ways to improve the performance of his team and is willing to take some risks. Over the past few years, he has dropped many of his conventional habits and become more and more technique based at the expense of yardage.

Jim wanted to see some of my kids demonstrate drills we use and give some explanations. I had my three captains and three more veterans demonstrate our drill progressions while his kids watched. The highlight for me came when we split his swimmers into two groups, long axis and short axis and with his approval, I turned the coaching over to my kids. I put three of them with each group and told them they were on their own to coach the things they felt were most beneficial.

It is a real credit to Jim that he would be willing to give up some control and let my swimmers take charge.

It was a thrill to me to watch them model, give specific feedback and provide excellent coaching from an insider's viewpoint with a totally positive and enthusiastic manner. I am sure that Jim's swimmers benefited, and hope that it helped my swimmers to realize what an intricate knowledge of their art they have.

I have never been more proud of any of my swimmers. It made me realize the tremendous benefit of making swimmers an integral part of the coaching process. At the same time, I regret the missed opportunities in the past because I was so convinced that it was my job as coach to impose every aspect of training the way I wanted it done, with very little input from the swimmers.

I am starting to realize that by being more open to ideas and feedback I have not only helped them to become more involved and interested in what they do, but also added a tremendous amount to my understanding of swimming.

It's almost a Zen riddle – How does one achieve greater power as a coach? The answer as I see it is that to give up perceived power and control, that which has added to the genuine power I have as a coach – knowledge. It has the additional benefit that giving the swimmers more input and ownership of the program decreases the necessity of wielding power as a club for control.

I did a PowerPoint presentation on goal setting this week, and we had a discussion about establishing good goals. We will have a season goal and then weekly performance, process, and team goals. We decided on Monday as a day to meet and work on goals. The swimmers are to think about their goals and then write them and share them with each other this week so that they can better support each other in achieving their goals.

One Step Back, Two Steps Forward

We did the following set:

Fistgloves

20 x 50 on: 45

or

16 x 50 on 1:00

Instructions were to start easy and as the set progressed, relax and lengthen more. If they were struggling as indicated by high heart rate, breathing rate, or deteriorating strokes, they were to sit one out. There was no penalty for missing a repeat. The challenge was to go as easily and effortlessly as possible. Going all of the repeats at :44 was perfectly acceptable.

As I suspected it would be, the set was a dismal failure. It was a failure for a positive reason, but a failure nonetheless. The plain truth is that most of them failed because they tried too hard. As they fatigued, their stroke rates, breathing rates, and heart rates skyrocketed. Red, gasping faces abounded.

When the set was over, we spent a great deal of time talking about why the set was such a dismal failure. People were so intent on making the interval that they forgot all of the things we had devoted ourselves to during practice. I made sure to tell them that I was exceedingly pleased at the effort, but let them know that from my perspective, it is far more important to use the mind and pay attention to how we move through the water and not just how fast.

I had them take the gloves off and try the same set again with much better results. My better kids continued to swim easily and effortlessly and made all the intervals. The swimming quality of the rest of the group was vastly improved, and many of them sat one or two swims out in order to maintain ease and smoothness.

"This is baseball. There is no crying in baseball."

-Tom Hanks, in *A League of Their Own*

I have learned to adjust to it, but like the beleaguered coach in *A League of Their Own*, I have not found the proper admonishment, reward, or magic charm that will prevent tears. It is inevitable when you have highly motivated female athletes. Learn to deal with it.

I had my first tears of the season when frustration of one of the new swimmers boiled over into tears. She is an excellent swimmer, and is still learning to use the Fistgloves, she was killing herself trying to keep up with the others in her lane. It was doubly frustrating because the others in her lane were making it look so easy, and she was barely making the intervals. She was trying to hide her frustration, but I could see how upset she was, so I called her out of the pool to see if I could help her out.

I tried to make her realize that the people she chooses to swim with have been using the Fistgloves for years now, and to assure her that things would get better for her very soon. If she was just patient with herself, we would be patient with her. I tried to assure her that we were only asking her to do what she was comfortable with, and she had to go easier on herself and stop beating herself up about going fast. It's not important at this stage.

"To know what you do not know is best.
To not know of knowing is a disease."

-I Ching no. 71

We did an underwater videotaping session this week. We had the newer kids do a 25 of freestyle and the experienced kids do a 25 of choice – either their best or their worst. I was encouraged that a number of them chose their worst, because it made it clear that they understood the process and didn't let ego get in the way. The IMers did a 100 IM.

We decided to do the review of the tapes as a group rather than individually because we felt that we could all learn best from each other's mistakes and successes.

Before reviewing the tapes, I feel it essential to preface it with some discussion of the purpose of the group viewing tapes. All swimmers need to bear in mind that any critiquing that is done is strictly about stroke awareness, and that aspects that are being pointed out by me are reflective only of my perspective of mechanical efficiency and do not in any way reflect negatively on the swimmer who is making the errors. I think this is a necessary disclaimer because adolescents, especially adolescent girls, tend to be extremely self-critical. Also, this year we have a number of very good swimmers who are new to our program. I felt it was important for me to stress that my critiques were based on my interpretation of what is efficient and effective swimming and that it is presented as one possible way to swimming faster. Each individual must find her own stroke rhythms, lengths, and nuances, but I feel that every swimmer should give the methods we use a try in order to have another possible set of skills to choose from.

To illustrate the point I used the example of stroke length, the idea being that there is no single optimal stroke length for all swimmers nor is there a single rate for any individual swimmer in all circumstances. The idea of working on stroke length at slow speeds is that it gives swimmers an option while racing. It is far easier to shorten the stroke and increase rhythm in a race than to switch from a short high rate stroke to a higher rate. If stroke length is developed, the swimmer makes the decisions about how much of each to use rather than just relying on one.

Overall, the swimming was beautiful. I saw very few bubbles, which showed me that the kids had by and large taken to the no-splash rule.

Our newer kids made the kind of fundamental balance errors that I had anticipated, and it was beneficial for them to see the effects of bad balance manifested by heads disappearing from view and front arms rapidly dropping down as the front hand was being used as a platform to support the head lift. I think this served as a strong reminder to those veterans who have struggled and learned good balance that it is important to keep balance as a priority. It is easy to focus on the errors, and I made a conscious effort to always point out the numerous positive things that all swimmers were doing, and there were many more positives than negatives. It is critical that I remind myself to emphasize the positive as a model of what to emulate because it is far more productive than merely pointing out what not to do.

The viewing of our best swimmers on tape was a treat, as they showed so many of the characteristics – length, balance, rhythm, and flow – that we have worked so hard on. It was also important that they all could see areas where there could be improvement. I think it was critical to the new swimmers as well to see that great swimming is an ongoing process and that error is an integral part of success.

The whole process took virtually all of practice. As far as conditioning, the practice was a complete waste. As far as swimming fast, it was invaluable.

One of the newer kids didn't know what to say. A few of the other kids reassured her that there wasn't a right answer. She's well bred and reluctant to blow her own horn and the best she could do was "It was different." When I pressed her further about how it was different, she said, "it was really smooth." I asked her if it looked like a great swimmer swimming. She just beamed and conceded "yes."

I made a point of telling the kids that all the taping today was my way of giving them a real compliment. The tape doesn't have feelings or lie. It told them that they are great swimmers.

WEEK 3
It's Such a Burden to Always be Right about Everything

*"To him, Homer was a great writer,
though what his writing was about he did not know."*

-Thoureau

*"He may look like an idiot and talk like an idiot
but don't let that fool you. He really is an idiot."*

-Groucho Marx

The week began strangely.

First, my captains deeply disappointed me for the first time this year.

It is their first duty to prevent me from doing stupid things. I asked who wanted to come in on Labor Day, and about 20 kids said they were coming, so I showed up at 7:45 and waited for the building to open — and waited and waited. Any dolt would know the building wouldn't be open on Labor Day, and my captains should most definitely have dolt-slapped the back of my head if they had been on the ball at all. All the kids who said they were coming did so, so I decided to cover for the captains and tell them it was my mistake and send them back to bed, an idea they genuinely hated.

Do as I Say, Not as I Do

Instead of coaching, I went for a mountain bike ride with my son and my dog Gus. We went to my buddy Hitchy's place, which is a great old farm just outside of town where Hitchy and I hung out as kids when it belonged to his grandfather.

The ride started in similarly doltish fashion. I was suffering mightily on the long winding uphills and ended up walking quite a lot. I was getting angrier and angrier, as it reminded me that I used to ride these hills with much less effort, and occasionally get off to help push my son while running along side of him. Now, he is the one pushing me in a different sense, and the question has changed from how fast can I get to the top to simply can I?

I toppled numerous times because I couldn't avoid the small ruts that are everywhere. The internal voice was going full volume: "You stink you sorry old man."

In short, I realized that I was the total embodiment of so many negative patterns that I would be appalled at in my swimmers.

I realized this and refocused.

I had a day off. I was with my best friend in the world and my dog. The sun was shining and it was warm, and I was healthy enough to be out and exercising. Could life be better?

I did as Dr. Goldberg suggests and stopped the negative self-talk and replaced it with more positive thoughts.

I flew up the hills easily and effortlessly, leaving my son choking in a cloud of dust.

Not really.

I still struggled mightily, but focused on the challenge and remembered the lessons I had learned over the years — keep the upper body relaxed, keep the elbows bent, don't try to avoid the ruts, focus where you want the bike to go.

I reminded myself that I was in fabulous shape for a man of 70. So, if I can stay where I am for another 20 years, I'll feel really good about that.

Riding a mountain bike has many similarities to swimming. The most obvious parallel is the balance issue. We would never see out of balance swimming if the consequences for bad swimming were as immediate and uncomfortable as in mountain biking. The same goes for being in the now.

On more than one occasion when my son was little, he brought his friends into the house for the "hey dad, show them your great bruise" exhibition. The bruises and cuts were results of lack of attention, bad balance, and going too fast.

It is a good reminder for me of what we need to focus on in the pool.

We need to continue to constantly be aware of balance and work on maintaining it.

We need to focus on the skills that make up a good swim.

We need to focus on *how to* and not on *how not to*, to focus on where we are going, not on the ruts.

We need to focus going at speeds that are conducive to maintaining our skills and not crashing the water.

We need to know that skills are not enough by themselves; we must have conditioning to go along with it. Along this line, I am not too concerned. I feel that we have been doing a great deal of base endurance swimming even though we don't cover much yardage. The body doesn't know whether the heartbeats are generated from kicking, swimming or drilling. The heart just pumps to meet the body's demands.

Zen and the Art of Swimmer Maintenance

I had an interesting conversation with one of our most accomplished swimmers. She has shown great resolve and has had some fabulous races when the pressure was on.

She told me she was a bit uncomfortable with all of the talk about flow, yoga, and Zen. She said that she didn't really think about being in "the zone" (her term) to get there. She just focused on what she was doing and got into it. Bingo.

I apparently didn't make my point clear enough on a couple of things. I told her how pleased I was with her observation as it was the very essence of what I had been trying to get across. One does not enter a state of flow by thinking about being in a state of flow. One does it by relentless practice of the component skills with sufficient attentiveness to each one for its own sake so that the mind is free to experience performance with little conscious thought.

Another point I was quick to clear up with her, as well as the team, was my borrowing from religious traditions and martial arts such a Zen, Taoism, Hinduism, and Aikido. I am using aspects of these disciplines, but not advocating the pursuit of enlightenment through practice of any one of them.

In the first place, I know virtually nothing about any of them. I have been fascinated by aspects of each and have spent a great deal of time reading and talking to practitioners, but nonetheless, I am confident that my gross misinterpretation of all would bring howls of laughter from the serious master of any of them.

I use aspects of these traditions that make sense to me because they feature elements of physical and mental training, which I see as advantageous to the kind of relaxed, focused swimming we strive for. We use Yoga to promote core flexibility and slow, rhythmic contraction of the muscles involved, and breathing exercises to promote relaxation and consciousness of good breathing technique for exercise.

To me, the idea of arriving at enlightenment through swimming is demeaning to religious experience as well as to sport. I think that sport can be employed in the pursuit of enlightenment as with Zen archery, where enlightenment is the goal and not a byproduct of the activity, but to me, the pursuit of excellence in swimming is worthy in and of itself.

A Trip Back to Reality

We had a rough practice today.

It was an eye opener in that the less-than-committed kids were all there at once. I guess in a sense, it is like every teacher's open house experience — you see all of the parents whose kids are doing well. The ones who most need to be there rarely show.

Before school starts, I have always made it quite clear that practice is optional. Many kids have jobs and family commitments, and I understand and honor those commitments. It is just unfortunate that some of those who were there least often could have benefited the most from the intense drill work and easy relaxed swimming.

Beginning practice with the full team, we had to make the adjustment to more swimmers in the pool and a great deal of confusion with some of the sets we were doing.

We have 34 kids now and will have to split into 2 groups.

One of my captains came up to me after the practice and told me that midway through the 50 set, she felt herself struggling and reminded herself that this was fun and smiled. She said it became much easier for her.

We talked about this with the group the next day and stressed the need to enjoy what we do. We have to get comfortable being uncomfortable.

The next day, we all did warm-up together and Deb did intense drill work with the weaker swimmers. The main thing all of them are doing wrong is trying too hard and failing to relax.

2000 IM choice of 20 x 100 or 10 x 200

My son stopped by the pool while the set was going on. He sat, watched, and said, "Listen to that." I listened for a bit and missed what it was I was supposed to be listening to. I said I didn't get it and he told me to listen to the swimming.

There were 20 kids in the pool at that point, some of them far from accomplished IMers. They were doing a long, tedious set and not one of them was slapping the water, even on the fly. There were just gentle sloshing sounds.

When I tuned into the sound, it was like getting a massage.

I made sure to tell them at the end of practice about my son's observation and how pleased I was with the effort they were making. They are a very mature and focused bunch. What I was most pleased about was that I never made any mention of quiet when I gave the instructions for the set.

Next, Deb and I worked with the JV kids on balance drills, then moved to the single switches. I had them wearing gloves and fins with the instruction that they were not to kick hard. It seems the biggest problem most of them have is a failure to relax when they have the gloves on, so adding a little boost seems to cut down on flailing as a means of propulsion.

I met with the captains and a few vets to get input on what they felt would be the best way to have two practices. At their suggestion, we are having the JV begin swimming 30 minutes before the varsity for intensive instruction, and then starting warm-up and some sets with the varsity. That way, the varsity kids can work with them as mentors. Their practices will be only 1 hour and 15 minutes. It seems to work very well.

The captains felt that it was important that everybody practice together so that all have a connection to the team. Seems to me they arrived at a great solution.

The kids looked so good and felt so good that they chose to do the last 50 as a block start. I was adamant that they not look at the clock, because at this point in the season, getting a time is not very valuable; I wanted them to simply focus on feeling fast and relaxed without pressure from the clock.

What was interesting was that in the discussion after the set one of the kids pointed out that she thought the paddles were an "anti-fistglove." She explained that they felt great while they were on, but her hands felt so puny when they were taken off. Whereas the fistgloves feel horrible and make knuckles chafe, her hands and her stroke felt great when she took them off.

The consensus opinion was that the paddles were effective for working on this particular set, but as much as they hated them, the fistgloves were far more effective stroke teachers.

Thus far, the emphasis has been on ease and comfort so that precision could be maintained. I haven't wanted anybody to press at the risk of ruining technique. However, the name of the game is competition, and practice is the ideal place to practice dealing with pressure situations.

Stirring the Competitive Cauldron

At the end of practice, I surprised my three fastest IMers.

They had been swimming such beautiful, seamless, easy-flowing fly that I felt compelled to provide them with the opportunity to swim 100 fly for time. One was genuinely excited by the challenge. She has been working on her mental game and it was huge for her to get herself psyched and go after the swim. For the other two, before they swam there was, to put it mildly, a bit of negativity toward the swim. They reminded me we hadn't even done a 50 for time and here I was asking them to do 100. They were tired and sore and didn't think they would perform well. One of them reminded me that she "always dies at the end of these." I said that I was well aware of that, but I needed a benchmark so that next year on September 7, after a very challenging practice at the end of a challenging week, after we hadn't done any timed swimming and they were really, really tired and sore, I would time them again and see how fast they could go. That was all this time would mean.

I also had them go separately because I felt that head to head competition at this point in the season would not be a positive.

Once the panic subsided, all three performed admirably. One had a lifetime best.

A couple of things emerged from the experience. On the positive side, even though all three faded badly on the last lap, they all finished with great technique — no short arming or splashing.

> *"Facts are meaningless. You could use facts to*
> *prove anything that's even remotely true!"*

-H. Simpson

On the negative side, the thing that continually baffles me about dealing with high-performing female athletes is the lack of confidence that they exhibit in light of overwhelming objective feedback of superb performance. How is it possible that all four of the members of a relay team that made All-American experience regular confidence crises?

If I were coaching guys, there would be no problem with just putting them up on the blocks and saying, "let the best man win," but for me, getting the girls to compete against each other has always been a daunting task. It has been my experience that the guys are much better at separating their performance from themselves. They generally have no problem competing with their friends and often seem to relish it. Girls seem to be much more concerned about their relationships with their friends and seem to see competition as a risk to those relationships.

What is absolutely baffling about this reluctance to compete in practice is that it rarely manifests itself in meets. One of the consistencies with my girls' teams has been that the bigger the meet, the better the swims. We have never lost a meet because people folded under pressure.

We have to start stirring what Anson Dorrance, the phenomenally successful coach of the UNC women's soccer team calls the "competitive cauldron".

One of the soccer coaches at my school had loaned me a soccer videotape made by Dorrance, and I was intrigued by the manner in which he made competition on his team a part of the culture. He rated, scored, and timed many aspects of practices so that the women on his team got used to competing with each other and saw this competition as a positive.

Thus far, the absence of competition has been an asset, and the fact that the girls seem to be much more process oriented gives them a decided edge over the guys in a technique based program. We have to slowly brew some of the good stuff in our own competitive cauldron starting next week.

We finished off the week with a very laid back practice.

They did some yoga, then 15 minutes of easy pulsing with fins. After warmup, they did 150 IM's for the rest of practice while I videotaped 25's of each lane above water and then went over the tapes with the swimmers. Today, I asked all of them to go fast.

It was encouraging to see that even though we have done very little fast swimming thus far, the quality of the strokes did not deteriorate at all when the speed was increased. Muscle memory is powerful. All of the kids who did fly were very impressive. Heads were low, recovery was low and relaxed with very little splash on the entry, and all of them looked like they were swimming effortlessly. Both flyers and breaststrokers seemed to be anchoring better, but that wouldn't be confirmed until we did underwater taping again.

It was great for them and for me to see such beautiful swimming, and also encouraging to see how readily they could pick up minute errors in their strokes and clearly understand the value of identifying these mistakes without taking it personally.

> *"Go ahead and play the blues if it'll make you happy."*
> -Homer (Simpson)

At the end of practice, I talked to one of yesterday's unhappy flyers. I asked her why she thought I had her do a timed swim at the end of practice with no warning or preparation.

She was dead on when she said it was to see how she would react.

The conversation was along the lines of:

"How did you react?"

"Negatively."

"Did it help your performance?"

"No."

"What do we need to do then?"

"Recognize when I am being negative and then change it to positive."

That's a first step in the right direction.

I pointed out to her what is so painfully obvious to anyone remotely knowledgeable about swimming in our area — she is a great swimmer. Her name appears on three of the State Champion relay banners that hang in our pool. She had to start to believe that her name was there for good reason.

I told her that I believed her name would be up there three more times by the end of the year. I needed to find ways to convince her of that, and in my mind the objective facts should have been all that was necessary. However, I sometimes think they have the same effect as if I had used another famous quote from Homer (Simpson): "No matter how good you are at something, there's always about a million people better than you."

"What you do should speak so loudly that
I can't hear what you are saying."

-Marv Levy

(Note for non-Buffalonians: Marv was the coach of the almost world champion Buffalo Bills. He is mostly noted for the fact that he coached in four consecutive losing Super Bowls. The perverse way we see sport in America brands him as a loser and detracts from the phenomenal resolve exhibited by his teams to return that many times after such tremendous disappointment.)

After practice, the team is having a car wash to raise funds for the season. I have made it a policy never to become involved in these activities, and have always left it up to my captains to coordinate out-of-pool activities. Both of my brain cells have to be functioning at maximum efficiency to do a reasonable job of in-the-pool activities.

Because I don't become involved does not mean that I don't value these activities. I think that they are phenomenally important for team unity, and team unity is vital to individual success as much as individual success is vital for team success.

I have always left these matters up to my captains for a number of reasons. I feel that by giving them control and total authority it truly empowers them and relieves me of taxing the minimal organizational skills that I have. I have been blessed with great captains for my entire coaching career, and this year's captains are thus far doing a phenomenal job.

What is interesting to me is that not one of the three is remotely as extroverted as traditional captains are. They will make poor cheerleaders at our meets, but are providing what, in my mind, is the best form of leadership, which is through their actions.

Before dismissing them on Saturday, I made a point of thanking the entire team for their phenomenal efforts in practice thus far. I reminded them that we are a very good team right now, but that that should not be anybody's aspiration. We have the potential to be a great team, and they are consistently doing the little things as well as the big things, and it is having the resolve to be consistent in our efforts that is moving the team in the direction of greatness.

Craig Lambert, the author of *Mind Over Water*, discusses the conditioning/technique issue in his marvelous book on the art of rowing:

> One day Thor (another rowing coach) and I mused together over a puzzling fact. Ergometer scores, he said, could help a coach understand effects of training methods on the athlete's fitness levels. Other physiological tests could measure things

like a rower's maximal oxygen uptake capacity (VO2 max)-quantifying the ability to burn oxygen, the fuel for endurance. Years of intense training can build those parameters to their full potential, but genetic endowment ultimately places a ceiling (Thor called it a roof) on how much they can increase. Nonetheless, many elite rowers had shown that even without changing any of these scores and without altering their basic rowing technique, they could still get better at moving boats. What could make them improve so?

Thor hypothesized that with experience, the rower's *economy* improves: they can do the same work with less energy by becoming more efficient. When we perform an activity for the first time, he said, it takes a lot of concentration. But after 10,000 repetitions, we can do it with less physical and mental energy. And after 100,000 times there is even more economy.

As tempted as I am to rev things up, I am convinced we need to keep going easy and slow for a while longer. Ergometers are stock issue on most good rowing machines, but we don't have access to those. I doubt it would do us much good anyway. I don't think the amount to VO2 max and other parameters can be developed to anywhere near their full potential in 12 weeks. I think we will have more success going after the 10,000 to 100,000 reps of quality motion to improve economy.

I think I know how a medieval lord felt as he waited until just the right moment to take the hood off the falcon on his arm to release it into flight.

Practice of the Week — Week 3

Warmup set: 4 x 100 IM
SA strokes: Kick; LA strokes: Triple Switch

Kick 8 x 50 in head lead position.
Kick in Sweet Spot: 25 on right side, 25 on left. Focus on balance and head position.
Swim 2 rounds of 4 x 50 FR or BK
Descend 1-4 and 5-8 as an "effortless descend" by starting @-4spl, then adding strokes to -3,-2,-1 on next three 50's.

Swim 10 x 100 FR with fins. Interval: Go 10 seconds apart and start next repeat when 3rd swimmer in lane finishes.

Notes: This is actually a semi-drill — an easy fingertip-drag swim. I tell the swimmers to focus on a relaxed high elbow recovery and general ease/flow. We used the fins to promote relaxation and make it easier to focus on the drill at hand without worrying about speed. This was to set up the next set.

Swim 20 x 50 on :40 or :45 or 16 x 50 on 1:00.

Notes: I let the swimmers select the interval they felt most appropriate for them and told them to sit one out if breathing hard/high heart rate or if they felt their technique getting rough. I required no makeup swims. The object was to see how many of the 20 x 50 each swimmer could manage with ease and economy. This is essentially the same set, which we did poorly last week, but the results this week were outstanding. Virtually everyone made all their intervals, though some had to sit one or two out. I made sure to praise them for doing so, for following the instructions I had given.

Drill/swim 6 rounds of 4 x 25.

Odd rounds:

#1 SA combo 3-3

#2 SA combo 2-2

#1 SA combo 1-1

#4 Swim SA stroke of choice @ max of 6spl

Even rounds:

4 x 25 as 7-/6-/5-/4-cycle burst SA choice descending to race speed on 4

Focus on maintaining neutral head breathing ("sneaky breaths") at high stroke rate.

Additional Sets of the Week

As we are approaching the start of dual meets, we did some other sets this week to learn how to generate speed while maintaining form:

2 rounds x 4 sets of (3 x 50) First round with Fistgloves; second round without

Odd sets: LA; even sets SA

Notes: The focus for this set was turning on speed bursts at different points in the lap: from pushoff to the 12_ midline on each length of the first 50, the middle 25 (midline to midline in and out of the turn) on the second, and 12_ midline to the finish on each length of the last 50.

Following this set, we did four minutes of easy Head-lead balance for recovery.

(**Note:** we haven't done much "recovery" swimming yet as all of our sets were assigned to be done at moderate effort and should not require recovery if done properly).

The next set was very traditional. It was an experiment to see how well we have progressed with our ability to focus and maintain stroke. We haven't done any sets like this thus far this year. I usually don't like extended sets of this sort because they limit my opportunities to offer correction or encouragement and because they limit the swimmers' opportunity for learning.

2000 IM choice of 20 x 100 or 10 x 200. No interval.

The only wrinkle was that the fly was done as 25's going when the last swimmer finished freestyle. The instructions were to go fast on the fly and keep everything else at smooth speed.

We also did a great short axis set using fins and paddles. The kids are doing great fly and breaststroke, but many are still just pulling their hands back, rather than anchoring and moving the body over the hands. To remedy this, we did a set of 16 x 25 BR with fins and paddles. The goal of the set was simply to use the paddles to reinforce the idea of getting the hands and forearms vertical and pulling over them using the body. We talked about visualizing the navel driving through the anchored palms. We also talked about moving the elbows over the hands instead of pulling them back.

WEEK 4
Real Questions of Balance

*"For every thing there is a season, and a
time for every purpose under heaven."*

-Ecclesiastes

We are now "in season", and our purpose is to go fast.

The week began on the most positive of notes. We had started to do more fast swimming, and the swimming that Monday was superb, a great focused effort.

September 11, 2001

At moments like this, I keep thinking that there is something from my arsenal of experience that I can draw on to comfort and explain the unexplainable to the kids, but it always manages to elude me.

As the events unraveled today, our principal was determined to keep things going on in the most normal fashion possible, and that included having after-school activities. I fully supported him in this and told him that I planned to hold practice. It has been my experience that in times of tragedy, kids respond best when things are kept as routine as possible.

As my swimmers approached me during the day, I told them we would practice as usual. By the end of the day, our superintendent and all of the superintendents in Western New York had announced the cancellation of all after-school activities.

Many people in the school had friends and loved ones in DC and New York, and anxiously awaited calls from them to say everything was fine. One of my swimmer's fathers had a meeting at the Pentagon that day and she did not hear from him until 6 p.m.

My daughter works near the Pentagon, and I was spared the hours of agony when she called late in the morning to tell us that she was fine.

I kept thinking of the thousands who didn't hear until the next day, and all of the thousands who would get a call of an entirely different nature.

When we gathered for practice on Wednesday, I spent time to make sure that they were perfectly clear as to my motivation for wanting to practice on Tuesday.

There was no real point in discussing the events themselves. All of them had seen the planes careening into the buildings countless times. I told them that as much as I love swimming, its importance is nothing in comparison with the gravity of the events in DC, New York, and that field in Pennsylvania. One reason that I had wanted to practice was that the goal of the terrorist is to disrupt life, and, in my mind, ceasing a good and positive activity would be giving in to them.

I also wanted them to be together because they provide such tremendous support for each other. As a condition of the Johnson City meet, each swimmer was to write an essay on how participation in swimming has helped her to resist illegal drugs and violence.

Virtually every person mentioned team support as a vital ingredient. Many contained such terms as "positive peer pressure," and many mirrored the sentiments expressed by one:

"Teens often turn to drugs when they feel depressed or abandoned. I know that I will never feel that way because I have 30 girls on my team to talk to. I think that every person on our team feels supported by all the other girls."

It is an environment that all of us are lucky to have.

Key Points

To me, it is critical to maintain stroke integrity and timing on short axis. We virtually never do short axis repeats at distances over 50. At this point, we have had adequate rest for even modestly talented flyers to handle quite a few yards of fly if the emphasis is on body swimming. In this practice, that's about 1500 yard of quality fly or breast. I have learned over the years to *never* tell the kids to just swim down. It is as bad or worse than telling kids to just warm up. It is critical that the body always be forced to swim properly, or else it learns that tired swimming is sloppy swimming. Moving slowly and easily rather than remaining stationary is much more effective in assisting in the recovery process and it is important to give swimmers something to focus on such as body position, head position, balance, or stroke length when they are really tired.

We have had tremendous success with what Terry Laughlin calls the "4-gear approach" to racing. The strategy is to stretch the first 25, build the second, go all out on the third, and take no prisoners on the 4th. I have always *told* kids that I wanted them to even or negative split, but never *taught* them how to do it. We have had more success negative splitting and even splitting races since we started using the 4-gear approach. It is interesting that I have yet to see one of my kids, no matter what the talent level, lose a 100 if they were even at the 50.

In order to set the stage for a more competitive situation in upcoming practices, I read the following excerpts to the team before practice. It is from a journal I had kept three years ago when Martha, our fastest sprinter was in 8th grade.

It is now time to start adding to specificity and start moving kids towards preparation in their specialty strokes. The bulk of these practices come in blocks of 50's and 25's for virtually everything that will be fast swimming.

9/10/98

When the bus arrived back at school, I pulled my two best sprinters aside and talked to them for a few minutes. One of them got 9th place in the 50 free at the state meet as a 7th grader. The other one made finals in the states two years ago as a freshman, but decided to skip the high school season and train with her club team before realizing her mistake and returning to practice with us.

There have been no problems between the two, but I wanted them to think about the fact that if they continued to do what they had been doing in practice there was a likelihood that both of them would be in state finals, and it was a virtual certainty that one would beat the other. I asked them to look at the tremendous asset they had in being able to practice with somebody so fast, and to see the rivalry in its most positive terms. They could use each other to become stronger and as each is a source of the others strength, the relationship should be cultivated.

From the November 15, 1998 *Buffalo News*:

Galloway Nips Teammate by a Fingertip

Not all the competition for the OP girls swim team came from the other team at Saturday's section VI meet at Bert Flickinger center.

In a race decided by 1/100 second, OP junior, Beth Galloway edged teammate Martha Whistler for the title in the 50 free. Galloway swam a season best 24.57 while Whistler, an 8th grader touched in 24.58. "Can you tell we train together?", said Galloway. "All I could think about was kicking real hard and trying to touch the wall first. We were a little tight, because we had been practicing hard without a taper." Galloway and Whistler went identical 24.73 in prelims.

There was a great picture of Martha and Beth with the caption: "Martha Whistler and Beth Galloway share a laugh after the 50 free."

How could it possibly get any better than this? Two races, .01 difference, and both kids were laughing. They had obviously paid attention when we talked about using each other to make each other stronger. They had become whetting stones for each other to "temper the sword until it is razor sharp."

There is a certain elemental sweetness to this experience that any teacher would envy. (In the state meet that year, they finished 3rd and 5th in finals. In 2000, Beth was the State Champion in the 50 free, and Beth and Martha swam together on the 200 and 400 Free relays that set state records.)

We are getting ready for meets next week. One of the older swimmers asked if we could do a set of block start 50's. It was a great suggestion and again reaffirmed the value of including the swimmers in the process.

To set it up, we did a 15-minute fistglove continuous swim knuckle drag, which, without the gloves, would be a fingertip drag.

With gloves, descend 4 x 50 from − 4 and get time then do the same set w/out gloves.

8 x 50 max from blocks ez 50 drill of choice between sets after all 4 heats finish.

Instructions: swim fast

(The simplicity of these instructions is somewhat of a joke, as I am not a fabulous pre meet orator. That is generally the extent of what I say to the kids before a meet. Last year, we had a Finnish exchange student who taught me to say "&*>?~`," which is pronounced "ooowee no piashtee," so that I could seem more accomplished and multicultural.)

In the future, we will do these with some sort of stroke limiters, but for now, I think it would be too much to add another challenge. They need to think about one thing for now, and that is going fast. If things get a bit ragged, I will have to accept it.

I find that I need to discipline myself to keep things narrowed down to one or two focal points, because I often say things like, "focus on riding your front hand a bit longer and while you're at it, roll your hips more and increase your turnover and keep your head down and roll to breath and try to calculate the air speed velocity an African swallow would have to maintain to carry a coconut to England." This puts too many balls in the air at once, and not one can be juggled.

It reminds me of the beautiful alarm clock that my wife bought me as a gift a number of years ago. This marvel of modern technology has an A alarm and a B alarm with three different choices for each so that I can wake to any chosen track on my "25 Fabulous Polka Hits of the New Millenium" CD, a radio station, or an alarm with a horrible sound reminiscent of the sound that a cat makes when its tail gets caught in the fan belt of a car when you start it up on a cold winter's day. It also will walk my dog, remove unwanted facial hair, stimulate my abs, and make fabulous French fries. The end result is that while I am awake, I use it to play the radio and CDs, because the buttons are clearly marked and all I do is press them. I still haven't a clue as to how to use any of the 18 buttons needed to set the alarm, so I just wake up to the beeping alarm on my watch.

Live by the old KISS maxim — Keep It Simple Stupid.

I didn't know what to expect with the block 50's. It had been a traumatic week and everybody was physically and emotionally taxed.

The resiliency of youth provided a counter note to the events of the world. The swimming was beautiful and splashless. There were no harsh slapping sounds, only sounds associated with flowing water, harmony with the water instead of fighting with it.

The swimming was also very fast; some swimmers had lifetime bests; some were holding times that were almost 2 seconds faster than last years' times on the set.

Before the last swim, the kids did what they do so well — support each other. We talked about making the last one a race simulation to begin preparation for meets, so all swimmers not in the heat screamed, yelled, and whistled before each group got on the blocks. After quiet for the start, the pool erupted again into cheers and congratulations during and after each race. Swimmers in the water practiced celebrating at the end of their races.

Harmony, youth, health, cheering, support, accomplishment, celebration — if only this positive microcosm of life at the pool could be morphed to include the entire world.

I had chosen the opening lines of the Ecclesiastes quote at the beginning of the chapter as a metaphor about the timeliness for different aspects in the season. The rest of the verse became supremely fitting as a closing.

"A time to be born, and a time to die; a time to plant, and a time to pluck up what is planted;
A time to kill, and a time to heal; a time to break down and a time to build up;
A time to weep and a time to laugh; a time to mourn and a time to dance;
A time to cast away stones and a time to gather together; a time to embrace and a time to refrain from embracing;
A time to get and a time to lose; a time to keep and a time to cast away;
A time to rend and a time to sew; a time to keep silence and a time to speak;
A time of love and a time of hate; a time of war and a time of peace."

-Ecclesiastes

Practice of the Week – Week 4

Warmup set: Put on Fistgloves

4 x 100 IM
LA: EZ anchors with 10 flutters between; Focus on snapping torso to generate power

SA: Body Dolphin BR
Swim 8 x 50 FR
6 long strokes and then burst to finish on each 25
The focus is to maintain Stroke Length as you maximize your Stroke Rate on the bursts.

Swim 2 rounds of 4 x 25 LA choice; descend 1-4 and 5-8
Progress from–4spl to–1spl on each round of 25's

Swim 4 x 50 Swim Golf. Increase spl each 50, as on 25's set. See how that affects speed and Golf score. This set was the first we have done this season with an objective of matching time and stroke rates. For the first three weeks, we have focused solely on developing self-awareness–asking the swimmers to tune in acutely to subjective feelings for speed and effort. While we'll continue to do that, we'll now add more timed swims.

Swim 20 x 50 LA choice. Take off Fistgloves after first 10.
1-10: 1st 25 @–4spl, 2nd 25: 3-cycle burst then ez to wall.
11-20 Swim and descend to fastest possible time. Start at extremely low speed and gradually build body rhythm.

20 x 25 with Fins
1st 25: Hand-Lead Body Dolphins, trying for minimum number of cycles (pulses)
2nd 25: Fast FL swim
Take fins off.

Swim 4 rounds of 6 x 25 max speed in choice of SA stroke.

In each set of 6 x 25, swim 2 each at 5-, 4-, 3-stroke speed bursts, then ez free to wall.

Between sets, do 50 Drill/Swim in LA choice of stroke. The LA recovery between bouts of fast SA swimming gives both muscles and nervous system a bit of restoration.

Cooldown set: 10 x 50 choice. Silent Swim.

Additional Sets of the Week

Supplemental Short Axis Sets

3 rounds of the following: Focus on great walls – at least 5 dolphins for flyers and great breakouts for breaststrokers.

2 x 50 max speed on 1:15

8 x 25 max speed on :40

2 x 50 SA kick choice for recovery

3 x 50 BR

1st 25: 3up-1down, 2up-1down, 1up-1down

2nd 25: Try to complete the whole length in maximum of 5 strokes.

2 rounds of the following: Swim SA choice with a focus on a "fast-hands" recovery: karate chop for FL, exploding the elbows forward on BR.

1 x 50 on 1:15

10 x 25 on :40

2 x 50 LA Combo to loosen

8 x 125 Flow IM

Every stroke to be easy, smooth, seamless and splashless

Choice of stroke for the extra 25

Freestyle Sets for Developing Stroke Length

1 x 75 max speed. Get stroke count and time. This becomes base count for rest of the sets.

Swim 3 x 75 on 1:30

1st 75 at 50% effort @-3spl
2nd 75 at 70% @-2spl
3rd 75 at 90% @-1spl

1 x 75 @ recovery speed: 25 each of Triple Zipper/LA Combo/ Silent swim

1 x 75 max speed. Compare count and time with first.

These 75's were extremely helpful in getting the team to lengthen stroke. The emphasis was maintaining a "long vessel" from fingertips to toes and keeping the elbow forward as they anchored the hand, even while increasing core-rhythm. It has been my observation that when the elbow is forward, the stroke is far more effective.

Swim 4 rounds of 4 x 50 on 1:00

1 Triple Zipperswitch focusing on switch timing

1 @-3spl
1 @-2spl
1 @-1spl

Socrates Meets
Sensitive New Age

One of my Global Studies students brought this anecdote in to me:

A young man who wanted to become Socrates' pupil approached him. Socrates led the young man to the ocean and bade him to follow him into the surf. When the two were up to their noses in the water, Socrates seized the young man and held him under the water until he was on the verge of drowning. He released his hold on the young man and waited for him on the sand.

Gasping and sputtering, the young man asked why Socrates had done such a thing.

Socrates told the young man that when he wanted wisdom as much as the air he craved when he thought he might die, he could become a student.

I like the idea of holding tryouts next year. I have a suspicion that most of my swimmers would pass the test. I don't think my Global Studies students would react the same way.

It is what makes coaching the ideal classroom — to have students who, in most cases, are there because they want what you have to offer.

We are starting to study the Classical Civilizations in my Global Studies class. This is an undertaking akin to the 12-week swim season from start to finish. We cover the history of Western Civilization plus Latin America from pre-civilization to the new millennium in 40 weeks.

I employ the Socratic method in class on a regular basis, pumping the class with questions to draw on their own knowledge. I think that there is great value to having students become more involved, but due to curriculum demands and time constraints, lecture is a necessity to transmit information.

As I have come to understand the opportunities that I have squandered, I've gotten more comfortable with a Socratic approach to swimming in order to take advantage of the bright, motivated kids I have in the pool. They have so much insight into how and what they do, and don't need my detailed instruction at all times. I think I have deprived kids of an opportunity to learn, and by extension deprived myself of their insights.

However, just as in the classroom, challenges have to be highly structured, and there can be no doubt as to who is ultimately in control. "Come in and do what you want" is not going to be any more effective in the pool than in the classroom.

We did a series of exaggerated stoke error (see practice at end of chapter) sets in part inspired by Ryan Orser, the wunderkind of the coaching world. Ryan was the swimmer who converted me to a technique-based approach. When he was a sophomore, he contracted a viral infection that got continually worse. After getting clearance to swim, he was limited to 1500-2000 yards/day of easy swimming, so we did drills with him. The strange thing is that he kept getting faster and faster, dropping from a 1:55 lifetime best in the 200 free to a 1:50 in a race that I have always viewed as one of the ultimate conditioning-based.

This past summer, he did some coaching at a country club and couldn't get his kids to keep their heads down, so he made them swim a bunch of laps with their ankles crossed and faces down in the water. I asked him why he did that and he said that if they couldn't use their legs at all, they'd have to balance or drown. The only way they could successfully breathe was to roll. I tried this with my kids, who hated it, but kept their heads down after doing the drill. This reinforces the idea that, if you understand principles, the door is always open for innovation.

Teaching my global class about Taoism, I have come to understand that from that perspective, it is necessary to experience something's opposite to truly comprehend it. There is no dawn without darkness, no usefulness to a cup without its emptiness, and swimming with your big, fat, stupid head way out of the water for a long time, makes a neutral head position feel real good.

The kids, as usual, did a great job. When I asked for feedback, they said they loved it. They said the exaggerated wrong positions made them try extra hard to compensate when they were once again swimming right. They said the fly was great for getting the head in the right position to swim downhill, and the flat hips made them want to really stretch and reach when they got their hips back up. They also said they were really whipped.

Sensitive and New Age

Reading over what I have written, I notice that some of this makes me seem like, as I jokingly tell my daughters I am, a SNAG — Sensitive New Age Guy. Anything that might come across that way is learned behavior. This book is about is swimming fast. In order to write it, I have had to abandon many of the things that feel good and right to those of us who were behind the door when the powers that be passed out talent; we can barely hide our disdain for those who were in the right place at the right time.

A muscle biopsy of my body (finding a muscle to biopsy through the adipose would be a challenge in itself) would reveal that I am the proud possessor of exactly four fast twitch fibers, most of them attached in proximity to where I can sit comfortably on them.

My athletic experience has been to fill the roles that the fast guys didn't want. I have been a lineman in football, a distance swimmer in the pool, the pick setter/lane clogger in basketball, a long distance triathalete, and a bike racer. When I played rugby, my lack of speed and the fact that I possess the kind of looks that could only be improved with violent face-first collisions relegated me to the scrum where I could dig out the ball and let the backs do the scoring.

Any of the modest success that I have experienced as an athlete has come through grinding it out and learning to live with pain. When I started coaching, there was no bigger proponent of the Nietzschean "that which doesn't kill us only makes us stronger" mentality. The words "I want you to go slower and easier" were at first uttered with the same comfort level as "no thanks to the chicken wings and pizza, I'll just have a salad with low calorie dressing, preferably with a side of ground glass." I knew what was good, but I didn't especially like it.

As part of the practice, we had our three best IMers do 4x125 fly as a relay. The set went:

100 + 25

75 +25 +25

50 + 25 +25+25

5 x 25

The instructions were to go as fast as possible. When each swimmer completed the 125, the next person started, so there was relatively long rest, but nowhere near enough for full recovery. The cumulative effect of fatigue grew with each repeat.

The swims were not timed, and the emphasis was on recognizing the onset of fatigue and learning to deal with it by staying with horizontal body swimming and forcing a relaxed recovery when every instinct is to tense up, flail the arms, and lift the body ever higher while sinking the hips. The instructions were to go as fast as possible. When each swimmer completed the 125, the next person started, so there was relatively long rest, but nowhere near enough for full recovery. The cumulative effect of fatigue grew with each repeat.

In the past, I would have thought nothing of a set of 4 x 125 fly. If the kids involved puked after doing it, that was a good thing. If anybody really ticked me off in practice, they swam fly all practice. I could never figure out why I never had anybody who wanted to swim fly in meets.

What I have come to realize is that sets such as this have a great value, but only if there is a dimension other than pain involved.

The genuine toughness in swimming comes in compensating for fatigue by having the mental ability to force the body to go against every survival instinct it possesses. The instinctive mode says to lift the head and use the arms to push down on the water to get more air, bringing the body more and more vertical, which will make the agony of the "big piano on the back" last half of the last lap feel more like an eternity.

This toughness is best taught by doing multiple repetitions at slow speeds with an emphasis on ease and relaxation to promote muscle memory. After this has been done, it is necessary to ingrain these patterns at race speeds.

There is no way that a great race will not involve a great deal of suffering, and learning to deal with pain has a great deal of value. However, learning how to delay the onset of that pain through proper race strategy and countering the instinct involved when it does hit is far more valuable. A mind that is focused on how to swim is a much greater asset than one that is focused on how to endure, with the added benefit that the focus on technique will diminish the mind's ability to focus on the pain.

Sometimes, I just do things because they feel right. Sometimes they pan out. Practice started with a universal plea from the swimmers: "Please, no more heads-out swimming, our necks are sore." I hadn't even thought of the heads-up stuff as anything other than an instructional trick, but it had become a strong aversive stimulus that, in small doses, has its place.

I lied my face off saying that I had really wanted to do a great deal of it today. I struck a deal: "If I don't see any of your fat heads sticking up out of the water, I won't make you do those thousands of yards heads out swimming that I had so wanted to do." Our body position was better than it's ever been. Those stripes on the bottom of the pool were getting self-conscious from being stared at.

We did a great largely aerobic type practice today, and the kids did their usual great job. I am continually impressed by the quality of the longer sets. I can see people consciously working on their strokes throughout what could be wasted effort if it was done in a mindset that saw it as tedium.

An Obvious Answer

This week, while reviewing my journal of three years ago, I came across a number of excerpts that apply to what we are doing now.

During the breaks, I had different kids choose the drills we did to loosen up.

I made the shy kids get up and explain the drills to the rest of the team. One of the new kids who hasn't said two words all season had to stand with me and explain in an ever louder voice why she was swimming so well. What I was looking for was something along the lines of "because I am practicing good technique." She was going to keep it up until she came up with the right answer. She finally said in a very loud voice that it was because she had a handsome and wonderful coach.

I had to think who it was, and then remembered it was a skinny little freshman, who is now one of our senior captains. I gave her a copy of the excerpt to remind her of how far she has come.

At the end of practice today, we had one more 150 repeat, and I told all the swimmers that if Sara could answer one question correctly through telepathy, we would get out and go home. I wrote the answer on a piece of paper so that the kids would know I didn't cheat. I then asked Sara why she was swimming so well. There was a puzzled look for a few seconds and then a glimmer of recognition followed by grin and her response: "Because I have such a handsome and wonderful coach."

The question was way, way too easy, but I let them out anyway.

We never do get-out swims. I always want to have kids view practice as something you do to get better. It is never a punishment, it's just what we do to improve. That said, it was remarkable how happy these kids were to get out of 150 yards of swimming.

Hubris

Also from the '98 journal:

In many ways, this team is more race ready now than many I've coached in the past were in midseason.

Another one of those ways our karma always catches up with us.

The day after I wrote this, one of my resource room kids told me he had to write a story that was like a Greek tragedy or comedy. I got to do one of my favorite things. Most of my kids are pretty bright guys who are sometimes misguided and need somebody who can relate with them. Accident doesn't assign them to me. Some of them have experienced little success in the academic realm — too many people trying to build their self esteem without teaching them anything along the way. They oft times respond well if I can give them a little something to throw out in class that nobody but the teacher will know anything about, so I had this kid look up Hubris in the dictionary.

It said Greek — excessive pride.

We talked about it being one of the recurring themes in Greek drama and mythology, and how the crew on mount Olympus in spare moments between begetting semi-immortals with young nubiles, loved to unleash all kinds of nasty havoc on anybody who started to get a bit too uppity.

In retrospect I should have known better than to put the race ready thing into print. I can envision the scene — Hey Neptune or one of you guys, hubris alert. Widebody guy, bad dresser. Thinks he knows what he's doing. Mild smoting called for.

We had our first meet today and performances were genuinely awful!!

We had our first meet. It was déjà vu all over again.

It was an hour and a half bus ride each way and the pool was dark, making it hard to see the walls. The kids were tired and sore from Thursday practice, so the rational side of me told me not to expect much. Even after years of experiencing it, the first meet is always a disappointment after weeks of great practice.

Based on the great swimming we had been doing and knowing the hard training they had just finished, my emotional expectation was that they were all going to break records, maybe even a world record or two. That was the emotional side.

One of the frustrations of all this slow, precise swimming is that it is difficult to make the transition to actual racing. Some of our newer kids looked like they were doing synchro routines. Experience has taught me that this is an inevitable step to fast swimming, and it is a mistake to push the turnover end of things too much. It will come on its own with experience.

It was encouraging that even with the exaggerated low stroke counts, many of the kids went best times.

The rational side of me was very pleased. The kids were swimming with great technique, and all of our emphasis on starts and turns was very apparent. Still, the overriding emotion was one of disappointment in not seeing all of the great swimming from practice translating into end of the season times. I know I have to be patient and stay the course because the end of the season times will be there at the end of the season.

I Hate Always Being Right

After arriving home at 10 p.m., we were back on the bus at 9 a.m., headed for a relay meet at the Flickinger center. There were 13 teams attending this year. I was tired, and I didn't even swim, so my instructions to the girls were to just have a great time. Maybe I had the wrong attitude. I keep hearing and reading about the goal always being to win, but I can never quite buy into it entirely. When it is a big meet, you bet, but I think this event was one of the things that make high school swimming so much fun. We decided that it was a priority to get every one of our kids into the meet, so nobody swam more than three times. There were only three "real" events, and there were some great events like breaststroke, fly, and back relays as well as IM. We went into this with the sole objective of having a good time and going out to lunch at a great Italian restaurant we love afterward.

It is not too often that things genuinely surprise me after so many years, but I was shocked at how well the kids swam. There was no residual effect from the mediocre performance only half a day removed. These tired, sore kids lit the place up starting with the first event, a 400 medley in which our kids broke the meet record by over three seconds, and ending with the 400 IM relay in which they shattered the meet record by 9 seconds. Even my very best swimmers were close to lifetime bests, and many of the kids swam the fastest they ever had, and they looked great doing it.

We won the meet, taking 4 first places and 4 seconds.

I guess I don't have to be patient for so long after all.

Also from 1998:

I got a call from a younger coach who was at the relay meet. He was looking at the Total Immersion book on deck, and so we struck up a conversation. He said he was trying to incorporate some of the ideas into his program, and was using our swimmers to show his kids what things should look like.

I saw that same young coach, Eric McClaren, at the meet and he has become a great friend of mine despite the fact that he has learned new skills so effectively that his boys' team had pulled the upset of the new millennium, all one month of it, and beat our team. The year before, we had beaten them badly without using a strong lineup.

It had been a meet of mixed emotions, partially because they beat us at our own game. Their technique was flawless, and as disappointed as I was for our kids, I had to admire their efforts.

I just thought his paying the official to DQ our relay wasn't the best gesture of good sportsmanship.

His girls' teams have also risen markedly, to the point where we just edged them out to win the Medley at states. In order to win it this year, we will have to beat Clarence (Eric's team), and I know they will be prepared.

Balance

We were video taping this week and I discovered some tape from this summer of my dad practicing his golf swing. I called him up and went to his house to watch it with him while I copied the tape from my camera to a vhs tape.

He lives only 2 blocks away and I haven't seen him in 2 weeks because I'm too busy with coaching, teaching, putting holes in water pipes and writing a book. What lame excuses. It would be great to have a drill to teach me balance in my life the way there is to teach my kids balance in the water.

It's interesting to me that I can help him with his golf. I played a quite a bit with him as a youngster, and he offered up a lot of great advice at a time when I would only do things my own way. As a result, my knowledge of golf principles is very limited, but I started to see it as very similar to swimming.

My dad is in great shape for a guy in his fifties, and he's 70 +. He's really frustrated because he's not hitting the ball as far as he did 3 decades ago. He keeps trying to muscle the ball and swing shorter, quicker and harder. I taped him a few times over the summer and started to work with him on relaxation, core rotation, smoothness and lengthening his stroke. He's hitting the ball better.

Some of my swimmers were on the same tape, and I showed him a bit of some of the drills we were doing. My dad knows nothing about swimming, but has a great eye for anything athletic said "That's amazing ! They all look like fish".

I filed that one away for next Father's Day. No bad ties for that guy next year.

Practice of the Week — Week 5

Warmup set:

4 x 100 IM

SA: @ max of 7 spl

LA: LA Combo 4FR3BK with a somersault on stroke transition

Here we emphasized length on the SA strokes. After 7 strokes, they kick to the wall. The somersaulting on LA is a balance challenge and a turn rehearsal.

8 x 50 Silent Swim. Build each 25

The emphasis is on building speed smoothly. Staying "silent" as you go faster is one of the best puzzles a swimmer can work on solving. They ALWAYS improve their efficiency when they do.

2 x 4 x 25 Choice of stroke

Descend time 1-4 and 5-8; Maintain constant stroke count.

The challenge is to combine cleverness and physicality. Find ways to go faster with smooth, effective application of power and by "sneaking" through the water.

Do 3 rounds of the following: First round with Fistgloves

Swim 5 X 100 FR + 4 x 100 IM

On FR, hold fastest possible time @-2spl on 1-3, then swim at least 500 pace on 4 and 5 with whatever count necessary.

On IM Hold @-3 spl for LA and max of 7S/L on SA.

Notes: The task in this set is to maintain pace and stroke length, then change speed while holding length. At this point, I don't think the kids have enough sense of pace to hold both time and stroke count on all five of the 100's, so for the last two it's just time that matters. In a racing situation, they'll have to sacrifice some length for speed as they fatigue. If I have them experiment to find the best rate/stroke length combinations for the race length and fatigue, they'll be able to do that in a more informed way. As the season progresses, I'll probably ask them to hold their stroke length for all five and then drop the interval.

The 4 x 100 IM's are recovery, but even in that, the kids have to think of ways to generate more speed at low stroke counts, holding @-3spl keeps it a mental exercise in efficiency.

Swim 16 x 25

Pushoff with no kick, then build the swim.

Notes: This is a brief recovery set with a dual emphasis. Distance and speed off the wall is critical to all good swimming, but especially so with distance swimmers, many of whom have no aerobic swimming base after not swimming since the conclusion of the last season, nine months ago. The no-kick pushoff makes them find their balance. Then building the 25 teaches the ability to change rhythms, which is critical in racing. It's important to emphasize that all rhythm changes happen by moving the core of the body faster, not by cranking turnover speed of the arms. This is not instinctive, so we rehearse and imprint that action ceaselessly.

Swim 3 rounds of the following:

1 x 100 IM. Work on flow.

1 x 100 BK @ 80% effort. Work on rhythmic core-body rotation.

1 x 100 FR (as 4 x 25 on :30). Work through 4 "gears".

Notes: The focus is to use the first 2 x 100 as a setup/recovery to make the 100 FR the focus of each round. The IM is to be done with an emphasis on smoothness. The flow we're seeking is a seamless, seemingly effortless interconnectcdness of each stroke. Because they swim all four strokes in each IM, this should rejuvenate the entire body as well as providing different awareness. In the BK 100, the focus is just to take their awareness of tempo from the arms — where it is instinctively — to the core body. The 4-gear 100's are race simulation. It has worked well for the swimmers to envision themselves as shifting gears as they move through the race — stretch out, build, sprint, hang on.

"Stroke-error" Sets

This is not a type of set we do very often, but I think there is great value in it. I would never have done a workout like this in the past because I always wanted swimming to be as close to perfect form as possible. I thought drills would ingrain too many bad habits, so when we worked on technique we did regular stroke at slow speeds.

Sets of 20 x 25 @ 100% effort

Odd 25's: Do something wrong on purpose
Even 25's: perfect swimming

Set 1: FL

On the odd 25's, we swam with a high head position and a neutral position — "sneaky breath" on the evens.

Loosen 4 x 25 ez Focus on swimming down the tube.

Set 2: BK

On the odd 25's, flat swimming, no hip rotation big kick and fast turnover.

Loosen 4 x 25 Dolphin Breast; work on swimming downhill.

Set 3: BR

On the odd 25's, swim with fist closed and head out.

Loosen 4 x 25 kick in Skating position; roll to breathe.

Set 4: FR

Odds: Taking a cue from Ryan Orser, wunderkind of the coaching world, we swim with legs crossed at ankles, using head and torso to balance.

WEEK 6
One Size Doesn't Fit All

Another Greek myth:

The legend of Procrustes

Procrustes, was a legendary robber in ancient Attica. He lived in the area of Eleusis, and preyed upon victims by inviting them to sleep in a special bed which he guaranteed would fit any person perfectly. If his guests were short, he stretched their limbs until they would fit. If they were too tall, he placed them on the bed and lopped off the parts that were too long.

I think sometimes we as coaches have operated in the same mold as Procrustes. We have found what works for a few very talented swimmers, and tried to train all of the other swimmers to fit in that mold.

All I Ever Needed to Know I Learned from Kindergarteners

The weather is turning here and I went out in the woods with my dog. I saw a V of geese heading south and was reminded of my stint working at a daycare center in Rochester NY.

It always seemed to me that one of the best life skills people can learn is to have a sense of humor, so joke telling was a regular part of daily routine. I would read the kids jokes and riddles, and they would tell their own great jokes like, "What has four wheels and flies?" I would say things like "a garbage truck" and they would delight in telling me that I was wrong and the answer was obvious — "a house."

We did serious stuff, too.

One day while out on a nature walk to look at some seasonal changes and to collect some leaves for a project, a flock of Canada Geese flew over heading south. I asked the class "Why do geese fly south for the winter?" In unison they all yelled, "Because it's too far to walk." It was perfect.

This was not the answer that I was looking for. It didn't fit into what I wanted at that time, which was an introduction to science and analysis, learning cause and effect and migration and seasonal changes. They should have known that I was trying to be serious, but the Procrustes bed I made out for them was just not the right size. Instead of chopping heads or stretching bodies, I needed to get a different bed for the situation.

One day the director and social worker came up to me and told me that I was getting a new student, Jimmy, who had one of those horrendous life situations that I can't really begin to comprehend. He had some autistic tendencies, which meant that he had minimal communication skills. They told me that if he was going to be successful in making a transition into "normal" life, it was essential that I be firm and consistent.

At the time, I was the only member of the Rochester Aardvarks rugby team who taught kindergarten, so I figured that this would be a piece of cake. I thought the big challenge would be to keep him from being afraid of me. This big guy with the black eye would just tell him to do things and he would instantly respond because of my size and presence, so I could spend all of my time being nice to the kid and giving him the kind of attention he needed and deserved.

There was a wading pool the kids used everyday after nap time (can you imagine how sweet life would be if all the people in charge *made* us take a nap after lunch every day?). The kids left their clothes on the cots after they changed into their suits. Jimmy was tiny and thin, and quickly chilled, and came up to me and said "Jimmy cold." So, I took him in to the room, put him next to a cot and told him to put his clothes on. He came running out of the room stark naked, so I grabbed him, took him to a cot, and told him to get those clothes on now. He got upset and kept protesting no, no, no. I showed immense resolve and would not budge on my demands that he put his clothes on; eventually he did. When I took him by the hand and led him outside just as the rest of the kids were coming in, he was still agitated and upset.

Immediately the first kid in line asked, "Mr. Aungst, why does Jimmy have Doug's clothes on?"

It seems on many levels that we have ideas of how kids should be and we want to tell them what we know will work, because after all, we are experts, and it is the job of an expert to impress people with what he knows.

Thus far in the season, I have not done a very good job of impressing the kids with the idea that it is up to each of them to make choices about how they swim. Because we have done so much slow, precise swimming, most of the less experienced kids seem to feel that slow, precise swimming is still called for in meets. I haven't impressed upon them that outside of a few non negotiables such as turns and streamlines, the idea is to experiment with lots of different stroke rates to see which one fits the individual best. The reason we do so much swimming at different stroke counts is not to prescribe a low rate distance per stroke for all individuals, but to give kids an option of choosing lower rates if that works for them. The idea is not to provide a single bed like Procrustes and fit the kids to the bed, but to provide lots of beds and have the kids choose the one that fits their circumstances the best.

This is the kind of week that makes high school swimming unique. We have a meet on Tuesday and Thursday, a travel day on Friday and a meet on Saturday. Try and figure out how that fits into macrocycles and microcycles.

I recently read a book for a full-year training program, and it mentioned a period of 16 weeks for preseason work. It's week 6, and we're almost halfway through our season already.

In some sense, it's easy to prepare for the meets. We're not going to do anything differently in practice, and will use the meets as a laboratory to experiment with different strategies and techniques.

My message has been "Just do what you've been doing." Focusing on the perfect practices will have far more impact on how we race than focusing on meets.

I talked to my friend Walt, the volleyball coach. His teams are perennial champs, but they had lost a game the other night that they clearly should have won. They had played sloppy, trying to kill the ball. He said that the next day, the kids were expecting a torturous practice, but he got out archery targets and placed them in various spots in the court. He told the kids to practice hitting balls at them as slowly, perfectly, and easily as possible. The next night they destroyed the 4th ranked team in our area 15-2, 15-3. He said he never saw the kids hit the ball harder. I know nothing about volleyball other than that I broke my ankle playing it, but it certainly seems like he has taken a sensible approach.

When I asked him how he would have handled the situation when he was younger, he said that there was no question he would have had a death practice. There would have been abundant suffering to atone for all the misdeeds of the night before.

There's something innate about the "that which doesn't kill us" approach that has a visceral hold on guys. I still sometimes have my moments of doubt about moving away from it, even at my advanced age.

We have a very unusual situation. One of our new kids is a very talented distance swimmer who started the season nursing extremely sore shoulders. They were so bad that she was unable to complete during her USS summer season. Fortunately, she is extremely bright and positive, and so has chosen to *practice* with unrelenting focus and precision at slow speeds and get out and ice whenever possible. I keep trying to reassure her that her season is not lost. She is doing herself a big favor by choosing to focus on what she can do, and doing it the best she can instead of whining about what she can't do.

In my early years, it seemed that virtually all swimmers suffered from swimmer's shoulder to some degree. In many programs, this would be normal, but here it's a rarity. The more we have gotten into body driven swimming, the fewer shoulder injuries we've had. It seems to me that the workload is spread over a wider group of larger muscles. The rotator cuff and shoulder joint muscles can do what they were designed to do — stabilize the shoulder joint — while other muscles and the momentum generated by the body core do the bulk of the work. We have not had a serious shoulder problem in years. If our experience is typical, it will be a great thing for the sport and athletes when a body driven approach becomes mainstream at the younger age groups.

When I asked Glenn Mills, a former Olympian who endured two and three-a-day workouts for years, why his body didn't break down, he said that he and the other elite swimmers he trained with were such great natural athletes that they sensed how to get through practice with an injury by making slight changes in a pull or kick to favor the uninjured joints and muscles. Those without that awareness disintegrated and fell by the wayside.

Once again, this is something that the elites can do by instinct, but the other 98% need some help with to avoid serious injury. Developing more kinesthetic awareness in swimmers through drilling and perfect swimming at slow speeds might open up the elite levels to more of them.

We are still in a slow-mo mode, and we have to break out of the low cycle rate rut. I used to think that just racing would do it, but it doesn't seem to me that there is enough time to let it develop naturally. We need to give it a little boost.

It seems that we have brought team unity to a new level by having the short, the tall, the thin and the thickly muscled use essentially the same cadence in all of their races. I would much prefer the lower cadences for now, but even though I know most of them will eventually find their own groove, it is frustrating because I know if we over stress it at this point, the results will be sloppy short stroke swimming.

The idea is that each swimmer must adapt a range of stroke rates to suit her needs.

We only have two days to practice this week, so we have to make the most of it. Monday was largely aerobic, we had meets on Tuesday and Thursday, but on Wednesday, we raced in practice. I'm sure it's a crummy idea from a physiological standpoint, but it seems like something we need to do from a psychological standpoint. My intuition tells me the kids need to *feel* fast, and we have the luxury of having much more depth than the team we face, so we can compromise meet performance if it doesn't pan out.

The kids looked great for the most part. There were a few who reverted to arm swimming, but by and large, they were holding stroke and reacting well to the head to head competition.

It is essential to stay positive, but the realist in me said that we were not going to swim well in our Thursday meet. We knew going in that we clearly had much more depth than the other team. We hoped for some good races, but the adrenaline of a close meet would be missing. I knew everybody would be sore from Tuesday's meet and Wednesday's practice. Most were terribly worried about a heavy load of classwork that was starting to land on them, and I always worry about people getting enough sleep. We have so many great swimmers who are also great students. It makes me very proud that my swimmers have a stellar reputation among my colleagues, because most of them carry their great work ethic wherever they go.

Even though we are swimming in the best high school pool in the area, I had very low expectations for the meet.

It is a burden to always be right. As I said, there was no doubt in my mind that the kids were going to rock the joint from the medley relay on.

The medley started us off with a new pool record. The girls beat the existing record, set by the 1999 team that won states that year, by over 2 seconds. The prior record was set at conference championships that year; for us, that is still over a month away. The entire team caught fire, and best times abounded. Martha missed her own pool records in the 50 and the 100 by hundredths in each, as did Robin Lehner in her breaststroke.

A Legend is Born

Robin is the swimmer who is going to make me a coaching legend. The rumor started that this girl started the season with us going 1:30, but went 1:07 after working intensively with me for that brief time. Of course, I started the rumor, as I have always felt it was necessary to claim credit for the development of every good swimmer I have ever even said hello to.

The truth of the matter is that she just moved into the area and came in with a 1:07.

I am continually amazed at insecure coaches needing to claim credit for swimmers accomplishments. I am often reminded of the story from Bear Bryant who once said something to the effect of "When we do poorly, I did it. When we do ok, we did it. When we do great, the kids did it."

It was one of the best meets we ever had.

When I got on the bus after the meet, I told my team that I was dumfounded. I beat the quicker ones to the punch by making sure that everybody understood that was different from being just regular dumb, because that wouldn't have been news.

I was so pleased with the technical end of their performances, but I was even more impressed with the heart they showed in putting the soreness and fatigue aside and doing so many best times.

On the Road

On our road trip to the meet in Johnson City, the kids had a great time. I see my swimmers do so many wonderful and disciplined things in practice and meets that I sometimes overlook the fact that they are kids; kids who laugh and scream very, very loudly and often when they are having fun. They had lots of fun on the trips there and back, and my hearing may never return to normal.

They were talking about kid stuff like "who is hot and who is not" and who is going out with who and what everyone is wearing to homecoming. They listened to terrible music, unlike the Jimmy Hendrix, Cream, and Frank Zappa and the Mothers of Invention that my parents absolutely loved when I played it. It was such a stark contrast to the incredibly mature, focused attitude they bring to the pool that I was struck by how immature and näive they seemed.

I read Rudyard Kipling's story *The Elephant's Child* to each of my own kids when they were old enough — read it and reread it hundreds of times. My parents had read the story to me as a child. I knew every time that things would work out in the end and the elephant's child would return home to amaze his family with his new found trunk, but on the first read, each of my children worried that the crocodile would indeed pull the elephant's child into the great, gray, green, greasy Limpopo river all set about with fever trees. On the second read, the kids could relax a bit and enjoy the story more, because they too knew things would all work out in the end.

When I thought about it, it occurred to me that the girls on my team are exceptionally mature for their age, and for them, the most constant thing in their personal development is change. I have seen hundreds of kids wrestle with their identities and act awkward, insecure and traumatized by trivial things, but I have to remember that all of them are going through these things for the first time, and they don't know that they are not a big deal in the grand scheme of things.

As educators, we are always being bombarded with the one-size fits all approaches for dealing with kids. I was professionally trained to ignore negative behavior and focus on the positive. While I do feel that focusing on positives generally yields better results than focusing on negatives, my experience has been that ignoring negative behaviors only perpetuates them. Acknowledging negative is essential for growth.

One of my better swimmers came into the pool for warmup and copped an attitude about the hot and humid conditions in the pool and the fact that we had only one lane to warm up in, as did every other team in the meet. I let her know in no uncertain terms that I was displeased about her self-centered attitude, especially in light of the fact we were guests of people who had extended themselves to such a high degree. I reminded her that she was complaining without offering a solution, and in the code of conduct she had signed, she had agreed not to do that.

I asked her if she had a solution to propose. She realized her error, thought and asked, "Could we please open a door?" I asked if it would be ok with Jim White, the coach of the hosting team, if we opened the door. He said that he had wanted it open, and had only closed it for the diving. Once the door was open, conditions in the pool improved dramatically.

At the meet, Jim was talking about how pleased he was with using a technique-based approach. Watching his kids swim made it obvious that they had improved dramatically from a few weeks before when they visited us. I think his free relays will be contenders at the state meet.

He said that they were doing far less yardage than they were accustomed to, but swimming better and enjoying it more. One of the aspects he mentioned was that after working with our kids during their visit, many of his swimmers began to feel that adopting side breathing for fly was far more comfortable.

His observation was that after doing multiple pulsing repeats, the kids incorporated the side breathing as a part of the body motion with minimal disruption to the stroke. I agreed with him. I always discouraged my swimmers from side breathing because most of them lifted their heads and then turned them to the side. Now, I give them the choice as to what they are most comfortable with.

No Good Deed Ever Goes Unpunished

Oh yeah, we swam awful, but at least we were unified.

My 22-year-old son had volunteered to drive one of the vans, and the trip there and back took its toll. When we pulled in to school, I got out of my van and asked him if he wanted to use the phone. He told me he would in a minute, but first he had to fight Hannah and Megan because he was sure they had shattered his eardrums.

It was supremely fitting that we arrived home in the midst of my 13 year old's birthday party with 14 of her closest friends. Surprisingly, they were screaming and giggling and listening to really awful music, in this case remakes of Bee Gees tunes, which, amazingly, sound worse than the originals. He looked at me and said, "This is hell. No wait, it's worse than hell." I couldn't counter the argument. Both of us left the house within 5 minutes of our arrival.

At the meet, Jim had also voiced frustration about some of his swimmers "not getting it." I have serious doubts that anybody will ever come up with a sure fire method to get all swimmers on board. My general orientation is to focus on the positive aspects of things, but I reassured Jim that I had a few kids who on golf sets could neither tell me their time nor their count. They just were not interested. For whatever reason, they wanted to be a part of the team, and though I would prefer that their priorities be the same as mine, as long as they were not disruptive, they were welcome on the team.

This also reminded me that not all kids swim on a high school team to swim fast.

One of the kids on last year's boys' team had been in a world of trouble when he was younger. He took stock in his life and decided to turn things around, and I have tremendous admiration for his resolve in choosing not to associate with old friends who were, as he put it, "going nowhere" and taking charge of his life. He was a truly awful swimmer, but he wanted to swim well enough to try out for the Navy SEALS. If we had made cuts, he would have been number one on the list.

He made it into the Navy, but I don't know if he will make the SEALS. I do know he is willing to put his life on the line for the rest of us, and given the world's current circumstances might be called upon to do just that. Can I really condemn his priority setting?

I think that the more beds we as coaches are able to put out there, the greater the likelihood each swimmer will find one that fits. We might have fewer Jimmys wearing Doug's clothes.

give them a little boost. Most of them finished at or near best times. A number went substantially faster than best times, and afterward one of them said that she could now envision herself going that fast at the end of the season.

The girls had a great time at the pep rally, raised money for charity, and won the award for the best float.

The theme was tropical paradise, and they made their float an island. The older kids dressed as castaways, and the younger kids had tropical fruit costumes. I told them I had always really wanted to be a pineapple, but they told me no way.

They further hurt my delicate feelings by telling me I could be a whale if I really wanted.

Practice of the Week — Week 8

Warmup set:

15 minutes with Fistgloves and fins: Alternate SA Hand-lead Body Dolphin and LA Triple Switch. Do this super easy with an emphasis on relaxation and great head alignment. The fins and FG's are to help ensure comfort and ease.

Drill/Swim 4 x 100 IM on 2:00

Odd 100's: LA kick SA drill of choice

Even 100's: SA kick LA drill of choice

We emphasized "slippery" swimming for LA and "downhill" sensation for SA. At this stage I am giving far more choice on the drills as the kids should know what *they* need to work on and how they can do that.

Kick/Drill 8 x 50

25 Hand Lead Body Dolphin, 25 SA Kick (choice of FL or BR)

The emphasis here is to work on incorporating core-body undulation into the SA kicks. Breaststrokers also worked on finishing the kick by squeezing all the water from between the legs.

Swim 8 x 25 Descend 1-4 and 5-8 @-4/-3/-2/-1 spl

This is a natural "effortless" descend adding one spl to each successive 25, building gradually to racing rhythm.

Kick 4 rounds of (1 x 50 ez on 1:00 + 4 x 25 max on :40)

Swim 10 x 25 on :40 Choice of stroke

Swim max speed to 20 yards, then ez kick from flags to wall. The emphasis is on fast swimming to the flags. Twenty yards is only about 10 seconds of fast swimming, allowing them to keep stroke integrity and avoid fatigue.

Swim/Drill 3 x 50 BR w/dolphin kick @ recovery speed.

We emphasized sliding downhill with a neutral head position, using a long glide, but with fast hands.

Swim 20 x 25 FL with fins — 7 perfect strokes no breath.

Notes: The best flyers complete 25 yards in 7 strokes so I selectively limited some to 5 or 6 strokes. The no-breathing part applies only to the "true" flyers, and is intended mainly for extra work on maintaining a neutral head position. Many flyers lift the head to breathe, upsetting balance. We put constant emphasis on taking a "sneaky breath" looking down at the water. We added fins to promote ease and relaxation. The more relaxed the stroke, the less need to breathe. On fly training sets and in meets, all of our flyers and IMers have been swimming great relaxed fly, and this set was designed to further imprint what they are already doing.

Kick 3 x 50 on 1:30 ez dolphin on side.

Swim 20 x 25 SA choice of stroke @ max of 7 strokes /length.

Notes: This time, I had the flyers breathe every stroke to work on seamless breathing and to make each length in 7 or fewer strokes without gliding. When Richard Quick was coaching Jenny Thompson toward the world record in the 100 fly, they worked on seamless breathing every cycle. Both the men's and women's world records were set using every-cycle breathing.

Swim 10 x 25 SA choice of stroke on 1:00 perfect and fast.

Notes: We did these from Block starts for race rehearsal. I gave ample rest so they could maintain near-perfect mechanics and timing even as fatigue increased. I think this *teaches* the body how to swim a great final length in a 100-yard race, though I'm not sure what this it does from an energy-system standpoint.

Cooldown Set: Drill/Swim 10 x 50 @ recovery pace: 25 ZipperSwitch FR/25 BK

Notes: The long axis recovery set uses a completely different set of muscles and nerves than the concentrated and intensive 1500 yards of *quality* short axis work that preceded it. Again, I never give a generic swim-down. In a short season, our time is too precious to waste valuable opportunities to imprint sound technique on a tired body.

WEEK 9
So the Renaissance Man
Says to the Chinese Guy...

We have been trying bursts in practice to work on rate. This means that we swim at extremely high rate for a designated number of cycles for each repeat. We have used it on 25's, 50's, 75's and 100's; the idea being to swim very fast for an ascending or descending number/length. For example: 5 x 75 odds 3, 4, 5 cycle burst, evens 5, 4, 3.

The key is to focus on easy, stretched out swimming after each burst. The kids tell me that they feel that they are getting more speed without getting sloppy. It certainly appears that way to me from the deck.

Oh No, Not More History

In my Global studies class this week, I was teaching about the Renaissance and was struck by the similarity of the Renaissance approach to art and the approach that a growing number of coaches at all levels are taking to swimming.

In the middle ages, there was a great deal of conformity. People were bound by tradition, and tradition governed everything, from how they dressed, how and what they worshipped, to how they made music or art. Individuality, creativity, and the study of nature were discouraged. Life was all about suffering well through long hours of physical toil and having faith in a future reward. Things were done the way they always had been done.

Similarly, the lives of coaches and swimmers have been dominated by the edicts of toil and hardship, and the belief that more and harder training is *the* way to the end reward of fast times.

It appears we might be witnessing a renaissance of sorts in the swimming world. The doctrine of harder is better is being questioned.

Artists, especially painters, flourished during the Renaissance, and what they chose to emphasize in their paintings changed dramatically. For example, landscapes, which had previously been seen as unimportant filler, became a central focus of paintings. Now, aspects of swimming such as balance and drag reduction are occupying a more central spot in the swimming picture without replacing the original subject matter — hard work. Of course, ultimately it's the time of a swim that counts, but along the way, grace, flow, balance, and position are vital components that should be given increased emphasis to get to faster times. Many Renaissance artists used classical Greek and Roman and traditional religious themes, but experimented with things such as color, balance, and form to modify them. The hard work paradigm should still have a very central place in swimming, but the way hard training is viewed, and the place of hard training might be differently applied.

Authors of the Renaissance began to write in the vernacular. Books and their new stores of knowledge became accessible to more that just a few elite. On the flip side, when there were only a few books around written in Greek and Latin, possession of the books and the ability to decode them gave those in power the ability to tell the masses what to do, which was usually to do things the way they had always been done. Many of the "powers that be" were not very keen on the idea of the printing press and writing in the vernacular. It gave the common (substitute less talented) man access to what the elite few (the 2% of naturals that Terry Laughlin speaks of) were privy to because of what they were born into (substitute genetic gifts for social standing).

Training in swimming seems to be moving out of the domain of taking what has worked for the elites, the "naturals," and applying it to the masses. Now, the less privileged (i.e., less talented) can look forward to learning ways to swim that will accommodate individual styles. In addition, for a technique-based program to succeed, swimmers must be more than blindly obedient — it is critical that they be educated about what they are doing, so that they can contribute to the process.

Renaissance painters went through an arduous apprenticeship, during which they spent endless hours practicing skills such as use of perspective by learning about horizon lines, vanishing points, balance, etc. Once these requisite skills were mastered, the artist was free to start developing his own representations of the 3-D world on 2 dimensions. The great ones like Da Vinci had more talent and produced masterpieces, but the less talented guys could paint more lifelike and realistic paintings than they had before. Some of these lesser talents put perspective into use as cartographers to make better maps, including ones of the new world.

I think working in added dimensions and perspectives might help us to move swimming into a new world. Not all swimmers are ever going to swim like Popov, but with someone to help them master specific techniques (rather than the ability to endure mega yardage workouts), each can develop her own talent to a greater degree.

Sprinters

One of the issues I have begrudgingly come to grips with is the coaching of sprinters. If we were in medieval times, people like me would at best be artisans or stone masons who could produce great works through hard work. The sprinters would be the Michaelangelos and Boticellis who were capable of producing the genuine masterpieces with seemingly little effort. It sounds like something I might admit at the opening of a 12-step meeting of some sort, but now I love coaching sprinters.

I think I, and others who were distance people because we had less than 2 fast twitch fibers in our bodies, have long held a certain disdain for sprinters. For me, it was always a showdown similar to Protestant Ethic vs. Hedonism. If Aesop wrote swimming fables, there is no question who the hard working ants and shiftless grasshoppers would be.

Distance people work really hard all the time because it is the right thing to do. Those morally lax characters in the sprint lanes are the epitome of sloth during workouts, even though it was us distance guys who displayed true sloth in the events under 200 yards. In the past, I was accustomed to the sprinters doing the same workout as the rest of the team, but by the time they got done with goggle and suit adjustments, going to the bathroom (I could never understand why they all had such tiny bladders), and nurturing the numerous excruciatingly painful injuries that required stretching, they did only about half of it.

Reality eventually set in when, after many years, I took a serious look at the events of a high school meet and realized that only 3 of them were longer than 100 yards. That leaves five events plus 3 relays that must be manned by the wretched refuse.

I realized I had no choice but to coach people to sprint. What started as a chore that I embraced with all the enthusiasm reserved for the end of the season cleanup of the outhouse at the family cottage, has become a passion. I realized that there was a great challenge and reward to *teaching* sprinters how to ply their trade, just as past masters taught their students the rudiments of painting and sculpting and watched the works of their students unfold into masterpieces. Fast swimming is now something we work on from day one. It's much more than something to do at taper.

I am starting to see this group in particular as artists perfecting each element of their craft with the creation of a masterpiece in mind. There is no lack of work ethic in this bunch. Most of our sprinters take great pride in the fact that they work as hard as any swimmer on the team. They work the entire practice, honing skills even during warm-ups and cool downs. With few exceptions, a visitor to our practices would not be able to identify which group were the sprinters.

I remember in my early years seeing a T-shirt that said, "When the going gets tough, the sprinters get out." I'm beginning to think that many of the sprinters I coached avoided the drudgery of my workouts, because they knew mindless yards would not make them fast. Maybe that T-shirt was a tribute to the smarts these people had, and not a jab at their work ethic.

At the same time, it has been almost 10 years since I had my last elite 500 swimmer near 5:00. I think excelling at 200's and 500's requires an aerobic base well beyond what is available in our season. That said, I feel that by teaching racing skills, we have had tremendous success in these distances in light of our lack of training.

The Renaissance was a period of renewed growth and interest in science as well as art. Both the scientists and the artists were held in high esteem, and in cases such as Leonardo, they were one and the same. I think great coaches are almost always scientists and artists. They study and employ elements of many different disciplines, but come up with styles that are distinctly their own.

An example of how a technique-oriented approach departs from traditional training methods might lie in the definition of specificity. Specificity takes on a new dimension with a technique-oriented program. Traditionally, when references are made to specificity of training, it is in relation to training energy systems. In a technique-intensive approach, this is actually a secondary consideration. The primary focus is, what can be targeted to improve efficiency?

One of the problems that I have with some distance-oriented programs is that the conventional standard of measure has been yardage — the more the better. In order to achieve yardage, most of practice consists of freestyle swimming. Drilling, kicking, and swimming short axis strokes don't lend themselves to high yardage. If one subscribes to the idea that practice is about training the neuromuscular system to perform flawless repetitions of the stroke at speed, then every part of every set should target a specific skill that needs to be developed while cardiovascular conditioning is occurring. This in no way eliminates the necessity of aerobic base, it simply gives it a different priority.

The idea of specificity is not a narrow one that would advocate that flyers, backstrokers, and breaststrokers swim only their strokes. It actually opens a door to a great deal of creativity, with the limitation that every set of every practice must have a specific skill developing focus. Virtually any drill that exists can be used to illustrate a particular aspect of stroke, but not if the drills are used as filler (swim, kick, drill, or swim with no mention of what drill to do) as they are in so many programs.

A set I have seen and used often is IM — fly/bk, bk/br, br/fr/fr/fly. This set brings up a question — what is the point of doing free/fly? No one ever does that in a meet. The answer is that if the focus is on balance, it presents the body with a different type of challenge than it is used to, and if the body can stay balanced in unnatural positions, it will be easier to find balance in the normal (remember, most of great swimming is not natural) swimming positions.

A creative coach can often invent drills for particular individuals or circumstances to target things such as lengthening, balancing, and side swimming. It is also rewarding when swimmers provide feedback about what they are experiencing in the water and suggest modifying a drill to achieve a particular outcome.

While reviewing Chinese history with my 9th graders, we talked about how the Chinese developed the most advanced civilization on the planet by bringing in advisors and scholars from all over the world and listening to what they had to say. Then, some misguided rulers came into power and certain emperors decided that China was indeed the middle on the universe, all that could be known was known, and new ideas should be shunned.

Then came the Opium War. Score: Ignorant Barbarians 1, Chinese 0.

Those who thought they knew everything fell by the wayside, and the learners took over.

I can't help but see some parallels with one of the local club coaches, who boasts of never having read Terry's book or attended a TI workshop or practice, yet felt qualified to write:

"In 13 years of coaching only two things in Total Immersion are really any different(sic) than what we (most of the world) have been doing anyway. First, lower the head a little. Second, a greater emphasis on rolling the body. Cut Total Immersion to the chase and it is simply DO YOUR STROKES PROPERLY! By 'canning' proper mechanics with a technical term (Total Immersion) we fool them into thinking they are getting something great."

I can envision this enlightened man as one of the masters teaching young Leonardo telling him to "just do that painting and sculpting stuff properly" and then going off to sip cappuccino.

The Camera Doesn't Lie

The video camera has worked wonders and taken on a new role as self esteem machine. One of our swimmers was getting extremely frustrated about what she perceived to be her lack of progress. The fact is, she was swimming as fast or faster than she was at the same time last year, but facts from me didn't seem to assuage these negative feelings. She is very talented, but had some distractions and hadn't been as focused as usual. This was also the first year she didn't swim year round, so she came into the season in worse condition than ever before. She had struggled and swam like she was struggling — no smoothness in anything, no matter what we tried.

For some reason everything came together this week and she swam great. The trick was to convince her. I waited until she got loose in practice and then had Deb tape one length of each stroke.

It made for one of those coaching moments we dream about.

Most times we do filming because there are things we are looking to correct, but in this case, we were looking for near perfection and got it. The vision of herself moving so gracefully and effortlessly through the water did more for her confidence than all the motivational speakers on the planet could have. *She* could see that she was ready to go fast.

I've come to realize that unless a kid is motivated before she comes in the door, she's not going to find success with me as a coach.

Before practice, I spend my day trying to persuade my kids to do the things that they need to do to graduate. I view my job as helping these kids to acquire essential life skills; sometimes, gentle persuasion is not the ticket and out and out coercion is necessary. I view swimming as a completely voluntary activity where essential life skills may be acquired, but feel if a kid has to be coerced, she should find something else to do.

While it's important to remember that there are a great variety of reasons to be part of a team, if at this point in the season they can't tell me how many strokes they took on a 25 or how much time they took on a swim golf set, they are not interested in swimming faster. I still spend time talking with these kids, because they're great kids. I just don't spend much time talking about swimming.

It does seem just in a sense that most kids who have put in the effort are swimming better and better all the time, but there are exceptions. One of my swimmers, Jonesy, is a great athlete. She is also a rower and a fantastic skier. She is not a natural at swimming.

Before the start of the season, I had a long talk with her. Last year, she tried to row and swim during our season, and I felt it was an unhealthy situation. We talked for a bit and I told her that she had to make a choice for her own good and that I would support whichever decision she made. I knew she was far more successful at rowing than at swimming, and was prepared for her to make a choice in that direction. It would have been a loss to the team, as Jonesy is one of those people every team needs. She contributes vastly more to the team in practice than in meets, because she quietly goes about her swimming and is always focused and making her best effort. Fortunately, she chose to swim.

I talked with her the other day about how much I appreciated the fact that when I gave her the option of swimming with the JV or varsity, she chose the varsity. I asked her how she felt about her decision in light of having plateaued for quite some time, and meeting modest success in comparison with her other sports. She told me she loved swimming and that practice seemed to energize her.

It appears that flow is not dictated solely by skill and extrinsic measures of success.

One of my favorite movies is a little known art film called Animal House. It is an epic Greek drama. The following is dialogue concerning the dilemma of the Deltas, the good Greeks, and their existential struggle against their nemesis Wormer.

D-Day: War's over, man. Wormer dropped the big one.

Bluto: What? Over? Did you say "over"? Nothing is over until we decide it is! Was it over when the Germans bombed Pearl Harbor? Hell no!

Otter: Germans?

Boon: Forget it, he's rolling.

Bluto: And it ain't over now. Cause when the going gets tough . . . the tough get going. Who's with me? Let's Go! Come on! AAAAEEEEEGGGH-HHH!!

Unfortunately, Bluto's impassioned speech does not stir the other Greeks off of their couches.

I think most of my attempts at motivational speeches to the team would have about the same effect.

We old folks have been weaned on a dualistic Western tradition of good swims and bad swims, positive attitudes and negative attitudes. To me, one of the real revelations of adopting a technique-based program is that it is necessarily almost Taoist in its orientation — good and bad are not separate entities, but rather, different opportunities to learn.

Being the father of three daughters and long time coach of a female team, I have developed, despite my best efforts, an incredible knack to "say exactly the one thing that would be the most upsetting," as I was recently reminded by my eldest. I have a standard line with my swimmers that everything can be interpreted in many ways, and if they think I said something that offended or upset them, I meant the other one.

One of the beauties of a technique-focused approach is that I am absolutely positive that if I speak to a positive or negative, or half full/half empty individual before a race about repeating the things we have rehearsed countless times in practice, and provide a few specific focal points for the race, there is a much higher likelihood that the swimmer will do those things than if I try to figure out exactly which things will tap into her psyche and try to provoke the correct emotional response.

I recently heard Megan Quann's coach talk about her uncanny ability to mentally rehearse races and complete them within tenths of her target time. I think it is this sort of thing that separates her from other mortals, and a technique-intensive program will help them, the less talented swimmers, the most. We know visualization can provoke physiological responses in the nervous system, but there are no guarantees that the negative swimmers won't be visualizing negative outcomes.

With a technique-intensive approach, in which the emphasis is on slow, precise repetitions and race rehearsals, there is no question that positive things are being imprinted.

I think this greatly reduces the impact of positive or negative attitudes.

I have also always been blessed by great leaders on my team who get the other kids psyched, and a great traditional rivalry with a neighboring team that always brings out peak performance.

There was a buzz and intensity as the kids are prepared for our big meet this week with that team. Williamsville North is the only team in our division to ever defeat us. The win/lose record over the years is about even, and we have never had a meet that wasn't tremendously fast and exciting. Last year, though, North graduated a tremendous group of seniors who played a major part in our failure to sweep the relays at the State meet last year. We got a first and 2 seconds at that meet, both times losing to North.

As this dual meet approached, it was interesting to see that there wasn't a lot of rah rah stuff going on. It seemed that there was a more intense focus on doing things perfectly. This is a tribute to the maturity of this team. There is recognition that there is no need to get pumped up yet. As one of the vets said, "If you can't get up for the North meet, you can't get up for anything."

The Crow Indians measured their greatness as a nation by the strength of their enemies. Enemies is not a proper term to describe the relationship the two teams have developed over the years, though. It's the best kind of rivalry that can happen at the high school level and we are exceedingly fortunate to have such great rivals to push us to do our best. There is an incredible intensity and competitiveness, tempered with mutual respect and sportsmanship. For me, Doug Cassidy, the North coach is the epitome of what martial artists refer to as a worthy foe.

I have very ambivalent feelings about the big meet, most of them centering around going head to head with my friend. Beyond having the strongest program in our area, he is a coach that every parent would like as a role model for his or her child. He has also been a role model for me. There is a tremendous amount of positive energy in everything he does. He is the epitome of class and integrity, and I know he will have his kids sky high for the meet and will have a lineup guaranteed to squeeze every point out of the meet.

In spite of his intense competitiveness and preparation, Doug says he doesn't care who wins the meet. He says he'll be just as happy if it's us. If anybody else said the same thing to me, I would say it was a crock. Anybody who knows Doug would realize that he is absolutely sincere.

It is clearly a case of wanting to win vs. wanting to beat, and it is clearly win win for both teams.

Interestingly, it would be very difficult to find two more opposing coaching styles. Doug is incredibly organized and efficient. He gives his teams long, fiery, emotional speeches, only he does them well. He also has two a day practices four times every week. He is very much into hard training, and his swimmers are tough and disciplined competitors. He is also very open to new ideas, and has incorporated some of the Total Immersion drills and ideas into his training sessions. He is not one to rely on doing only those things that have brought him success in the past.

Last year's meet was the all-time best. North beat us by 4 points, and three races were decided by a combined total of 14 seconds.

One of the most amazing displays of what sport is supposed to be about occurred after North beat us last year to break our 3-year winning streak. When the final results were announced, there were no tears from our side. Our kids went over and hugged and congratulated the North kids and Doug, and a number of them told me how happy they were for the North kids. They felt that losing a meet that was that close meant it was just how things were supposed to be, and they needed to pay tribute to a worthy foe.

I, on the other hand, didn't sleep that night, because I kept playing the meet over and over trying to figure out what I could have done differently. Doug still probably thinks one of his students was behind his car having four flat tires when he left for home after the meet.

Our meet this year was not close, but it was still very exciting — lots of people in the stands and lots of cheering from the kids. We again did many best times, and this year, we won.

I am pleased to see this, as I know we are still swimming unrested. Not one of the kids have tapered or shaved, and because we are significantly stronger than any other team we swim, we have been able to continue hard training without any let up. We have also been able to practice before each home meet, which is a huge advantage and a tribute to the maturity level of this team. They know that practicing before a meet may make them more tired and maybe not as effective in the meet, but they seem to have a clear understanding of the process, and know that we sacrifice some performance during the season in an effort to do great things at the end.

This is the end of our dual meet season and we finished undefeated. This year's seniors have lost 1 meet since they were freshmen.

We have qualified 21 swimmers for our conference championships, which is a record for us, and all but one of them has qualified for our Sectionals (state qualifiers), so they will have an additional 3 weeks, meaning we will be able to train hard this week and next before we begin our taper.

Practice of the Week – Week 9

Put Fistgloves on

Warmup set: 4 x 100 IM

Odd 25's SA Combo-3

Even 25's LA ez anchors

8 x 50: 25 Zipper switch, 25 build FR

2 rounds of 4 x 25

3, 4, 5, 6-cycle bursts, then ez to wall

Kick 4 x 100 max speed in Hand Lead Sweet Spot

Swim 20 x 50 LA choice of stroke

1st 25 Focus on SL and accelerate into turn. 2nd 25 Swim 3-cycle burst at max speed, then EZ to wall

Take off Fistgloves

2 rounds of 10 x 100

1st round: Start superslow at 50% effort then, descend time gradually to max

2nd round: (50+50) with: 10 rest to get time

Swim 1st 50 @–2 spl. Swim 2nd 50 at any SMOOTH stroke count and make sure it is faster than the first 50.

3 x 500 IM: The order for each 500 is:

25/50/75/50/25/50/75/50/25/50/25

25: 5 strokes max speed FL (then EZ to wall)

50: 25 ez BK 25 fast BR

75: build FR @–4,-3,-2 spl

Notes: The purpose of this item is to give the swimmers a "rate puzzle" to solve. The mix of minus cycle, descending times and max speed provides many opportunities to experiment with different combinations of stroke length and stroke rate.

Before the meet on Tuesday, we had an "extended warmup" practice:

15 minutes alternating 25 ez anchors and 25 fingertip drag w/small fins

4 x 100 IM drill choice

8 x 50 FR 25 drill choice/25 build to max

2 rounds of 4 x 25
1st round: SA 7, 6, 5, 4 Swim faster as number of cycles decreases.
2nd round: LA 3, 4, 5, 6 Maintain speed as number of cycles increases.

3 rounds of 4 x 50 Complete Choice
I am consciously giving these kids more choices as they know better than I what makes them feel good. I don't even concern myself with whether they do it or not because it is also their choice to come in an hour early before home meets.

Stirring the Competitive Cauldron

Hitchy just accused me of living under a rock somewhere because I was totally unfamiliar with the sport of ferret legging and the legendary exploits of Reg Mellor, the Michael Jordan of his sport, described here in an excerpt from *Outside Magazine.*

Mr. Reg Mellor, the "king of the ferret-leggers," paced across his tiny Yorkshire miner's cottage as he explained the rules of the English sport that he has come to dominate rather late in life. "Ay, lad," said the seventy-two-year-old champion, "no jock-straps allowed. No underpants — nothin' whatsoever. And it's no good with tight trousers, mind ye. Little bah-stards have to be able to move around inside there from ankle to ankle."

Basically, ferret-legging involves the tying of a competitor's trousers at the ankles and the insertion into those trousers of a couple of peculiarly vicious fur-coated, foot-long carnivores called ferrets. The brave contestant's belt is then pulled tight, and he proceeds to stand there in front of the judges as long as he can, while animals with claws like hypodermic needles and teeth like number 16 carpet tacks try their damnedest to get out.

From a dark and obscure past, the sport has made an astonishing comeback in recent years. When I first heard about ferret-legging, in 1972, the world record stood at forty painful seconds of "keepin' 'em down," as they say in ferret-legging circles. A few years later the dreaded one-minute mark was finally surpassed. The current record — implausible as it may seem — now stands at an awesome five hours and twenty-six minutes, a mark reached last year by the gaudily tattooed little Yorkshireman with the waxed military mustache who now stood two feet away from me explaining the technicalities of this burgeoning sport.

"The ferrets must have a full mouth o' teeth," Reg Mellor said as he fiddled with his belt. "No filing of the teeth; no clipping. No dope for you or the ferrets. You must be sober, and the ferrets must be hungry — though any ferret'll eat yer eyes out even if he isn't hungry."

Maybe we should bag all the Yoga stuff and include this in our dryland. We could revolutionize training with the three f's — fins, Fistgloves, and ferrets. I can't help but wonder how many of the grueling practices I designed in the past to "toughen 'em up" accomplished anything more than the providing the same sense of pride that ol' Reg felt at "keepin' em down." It seems that it is far more productive to give stressful sets that have specific focal points which allow rehearsal for how to hold technique together while distracted by some degree of discomfort. We want to strive for efficiency to stave off pain, because there is no reward at the end of a race for who suffers more, only for who goes faster.

We want the people in the other lanes to feel like they are ferret legging.

This Saturday, we hosted the B meet, a championship format meet for all the kids who didn't make the championship cuts. The coaches do all the seeding and officiating, and I am the official starter. There are also awards and team scoring. Not one swimmer has ever false started in the 10 or so years we have been doing this meet. I was a diving judge last year, but I did what I had always wanted to do, and threw some 10's; people were outraged. It seemed to me that if the kids were only doing 4 dives and there is no such thing as an official four dive score, it would beat the heck out of throwing the 1's and 2's most of the dives deserved, and they could tell their mommas they got a ten.

I have to make a special offering to the powers that be to grant me another year with no divers. My daughter is safe, as she just turned 13, and the gods don't consider sacrificing a teenager one has to live with a worthy offering.

The concept of the B meet raises some interesting questions. Are we really doing the kids a favor by having a meet in which the only way you qualify is not to qualify? Does this lower their aim? What's wrong with having x amount of time to make a qualifying time and if you make it you're in and if not you're done?

My kids have never liked going, but other coaches tell me their kids enjoy it. I have always run the meet, in part because I am so fortunate to have so many talented swimmers show up at my pool every year, and want to do anything I can to help others build programs, as we all benefit when the competition is strong.

I had this week well conceived in my mind. We had a meet Friday and were unable to practice on Saturday because of the B meet, so I figured we would work really hard on Monday and Tuesday, recover on Wednesday, and Friday would be easy aerobic, as we had meets on Thursday and Saturday.

Practice was cancelled on Monday due to a pool problem, so that forced me to rethink the entire week. I really wanted Tuesday to be a lactic tolerance day and to do timed 100's, but they were going to get plenty of that at the prelims and finals. So, I decided we needed a more aerobic workout.

I wrote a long, detailed practice and when I got to the pool, the captains asked me if we couldn't do the set of 8 x 50 max in heats one last time. We hadn't done it all year. They said the kids felt rested and were motivated to a great job. So, my workout went into the recycling bin.

How many coaches in America have kids come to them and ask to do a workout that is harder than the one that was prepared?

Of Birds and Men

When I was preparing for our Renaissance unit in Global studies, I read about early attempts at human powered flight, and saw many parallels to our situation.

Leonardo Da Vinci drew sketches in one of his notebooks. He had prototypes for a helicopter and a parachute, which would have proven extremely useful to pilots of a third invention, a flying machine called an ornithopter. It was a human-powered contraption designed to flap its wings like a bird's.

For some early aeronauts, those daring souls who first attempted to fly, wrong assumptions about flight were sometimes fatal. They observed birds in flight and tried to mimic what they did without an understanding of the laws of aerodynamics. By observing that birds flapped their wings, they concluded that it was the flapping of the wings that caused the birds to fly. It was good observation, but led to wrong and sometimes disastrous conclusions.

Early pedal-powered ornithopters were designed so that pedaling faster would make wings flap faster and thereby cause lift. None proved successful. These included the early attempts by the Belgian Vincent DeGroof, who crashed to his death in 1874. The way was paved for Wilbur and Orville only after an understanding that it was not the flapping of wings, but rather the pressure differential on the wings that caused lift. Unfortunately, these understandings came too late for many would be pilots such as the unfortunate Mr. DeGroof, who made a single flight off a cliff.

Ironically, while observations of birds in the air led ornithopter inventors to mimic them, the observation that most marine dwellers do not have long appendages like our arms led to the conclusion that human swimming must be vastly different than fish swimming. This observation once again led to wrong, though decidedly less calamitous, results. Human swimming, until very recently, has had little to do with natural motions of aquatic animals. Just as the assumption that rapidly flapping wings could cause propulsion enough for flight proved erroneous, it is starting to appear that wildly flailing arms to push water back more force-fully is also a failure to understand laws of physics. For years, it was doctrine for many well-intentioned coaches like myself that for humans to swim fast, the body must ride on the surface with the head raised and looking forward so that a hydroplaning effect could be achieved.

Aquatic animals are vastly more efficient at moving *through* the water, because they use their bodies to propel themselves and allow the water to support them. Even the blue whale moving through the depths of the ocean where pressure is far greater can travel at cruising speeds of approximately 20 mph, which is vastly more efficient than the fastest human with a whopping speed of 6 mph in the water; a speed that can be maintained for duration of approximately 20 seconds.

The early ornithopter pilots trained rigorously for flight attempts, reasoning that if they could generate more force, flight would be possible. I, and many coaches like me, have traditionally put swimmers through workouts with the same idea in mind. Until relatively recently, few people noticed that those swimmers who were the fastest generally also moved through the water with the least resistance. For those swimmers who didn't intuitively move well through the water, workouts were likely the equivalent of training harder to move an ornithopter off the ground — they could make some improvements, but would always be limited by an inefficient design.

The pilots of those early flying machines pedaling madly off cliffs must have experienced momentary sensations of flight before they realized they were plummeting to their doom. In past years, swimmers that I yelled at to crank their arms faster must have gotten a similar sensation and felt like they were indeed flying through the water before falling off the formidable, though decidedly less lethal, cliff created by drag and resistance.

In 1979, Bryan Allan piloted the Gossamer Albatross, a human powered aircraft, across the English Channel. I have no doubt that Mr. Allan trained religiously and put forth a Herculean effort to accomplish his channel crossing, but unlike the ornithopter pilots, he did so in a more aerodynamically designed vessel to take advantage of the support offered by the air.

Hopefully, what we are doing in the pool will create aquatic versions of the Gossamer Albatross. We must start to generate more power, but make sure we are doing it efficiently to move through the water, not fight it.

Similarly, it has consistently been documented that at every level, what separates the elite swimmers from everybody else is distance per stroke. In order to achieve greater distance per stroke, elite swimmers generate less power than slower competitors. They achieve better distance per stroke by creating less resistance.

I'm still concerned with stroke rate. I pointed out that we've done an exceptional job at mastering the slow and effortless part. It is speed combined with a *perceived* lack of effort that we're after when we race. We have to learn to sacrifice a little of the length and grace we've been cultivating to work up to racing rates. We are entering the competitive part of the season, and we will have to swim at higher rates. We just have to be careful not to end up like Vincent DeGroof.

On Wednesday, we gave any of the kids who hadn't made Sectionals the day off. They needed to be rested and ready to make their times. The rest of the kids wouldn't really rest for another week.

Knowing Thursday would be a tough night, as we don't start until 7:00 pm, I decided not to do anything too strenuous for a practice. We did some speed work and some aerobic work. The speed work was all in short bursts, so it left neither fatigue nor soreness.

The Scar

I was playing hoops and something new and different happened — I got injured. I caught the top of somebody's head with my cheek, and it opened a nasty gash under my eye. It bled quite a bit, so Dan, one of the young guys I teach with, came with me to get it cleaned up. I called my wife, who is a nurse to ask her if I should get stitches. Dan thought it was extremely funny that her reply was simply "Do you care if you have another scar?" I, of course, said no, and she said "don't bother with the stitches."

I thought about it a bit later and had to laugh because my wife is a very compassionate person, but my son and I have sort of used up more than our share of that compassion with too many exploits that have landed one or the other and sometimes both of us in the emergency room. I also remembered how terrified I was the first time I split my cheek open on the top of somebody's head and had to get stitches. I was tremendously worried about the scar it would leave, because I didn't realize that scars add character to a man and women dig them. (I heard or read that somewhere, and choose to believe it in spite a lack of any confirming evidence.) It is important to me that as I get farther and farther from my youth that I keep in mind how many things I now view as mundane seemed genuinely traumatic at the time.

An Unfortunate Case of Deja vu

From my 1998 Journal:

One of my kids came to see me. She had obviously been crying, and so we went out in the hall to talk.

When I asked her what was wrong, the deluge started and she proceeded to tell me about some serious family issues she was dealing with.

My swimmers are some of the greatest people on the planet. They are, however, a microcosm of society and don't live just in the pool. I coach in an affluent suburban district that is isolated from much of the ills of poverty, but there are some very serious problems that no community is safe from — deaths of family members, suicide, abuse, divorce, eating disorders, mental illness, and substance abuse, to mention a few. It's an absolute necessity for every coach to decide what role he or she wants to take in dealing with kids' lives outside of the pool.

My personal way of dealing with any confidential issue, (and believe me, to a teenager, boyfriend/girlfriend issues can be as serious as anything else) is to establish things up front and tell kids that I will never tell anybody what they say unless it is harmful to them or to somebody else. I will tell nobody unless they give me their permission. (When I make this promise, the only way I can keep it is to tell absolutely nobody, including my wife). If the problem is something I can't help solve, I will put them in touch with somebody who can help them. I will always be here to listen if anybody just needs to talk.

My advice to a new coach would be to think about some worst case scenarios and before a situation arises, find people who can help you get kids help with serious issues. Unless you are a trained counselor, recognize that there are going to be problems out there that you will be unable to help with.

I was fortunate to have the sage counsel of Bob Healy, a first-rate psychologist, for many years. He taught me about listening patiently and was always my go-to guy when things went awry with kids in my classroom. Most importantly, he also taught me to call for help when I needed it and to take advantage of every resource: teachers, counselors, psychologists, and the school nurse.

There are many things out there now that make choices more difficult for this generation of kids. Kids are the same as they have always been, but society is not. It seems that there are many more kids who have been seriously let down by the adults in their lives, and are looking for a competent adult they can count on.

One of the things I like best about what I do is that in the pool, I can teach kids to be more competent in one little area of their life and help provide the means for genuine achievement. The more competencies a kid has, the more resilient they are to the stresses and strains they experience.

This is unfortunately a scene that I know will be repeated every year, many years on more than one occasion.

This year was no exception and it was repeated yesterday. Different kid, different family problem, many more tears, and the best I could do was just listen. I'm glad these things still bother me.

Swim Lessons from Big Al's

Growing up in Western New York, you get used to jokes about snow and low-brow culture. Many of the more sophisticated people from Buffalo go to Toronto, because it has a much more cosmopolitan atmosphere.

When Eric and I did a swim workshop in Toronto last spring, we asked where the best place to eat would be. I was assured that it was a place called Al Gonquins. The décor was very rustic, like a cabin in the park minus the mosquitoes and black flies, and there was an enormous aquarium filled with native fish (bass and perch) and a number of turtles. I was heartened by a sign that said "Big Al's feeding frenzy every Saturday night at 8:00." I was sure it was an all you can eat buffet.

We got our table and had a few drinks while waiting for the feeding frenzy to begin. Soon, I heard clapping and cheering coming from the lobby where the aquarium was. I went out to see what the source of the commotion was and discovered what Big Al's feeding frenzy was. One of the employees opened a big bag of goldfish into the fish tank, and the patrons crowded around to root on their favorite bass or turtle as it pursued dinner.

The crowd favorites were the turtles, which were nowhere as quick as the bass; so, they had to adopt different strategies to obtain the fish, namely working the victim into a corner and then trapping it and scarfing it up. The key for the predators in the tank was finding what worked best for them.

Eric and I are going to surprise our wives and take them to Toronto for an evening of dinner theater. I'm sure that they'll find the proceedings at Al Gonquins as culturally uplifting as we did.

I know my girls would be less than thrilled to be compared with bass and turtles, but so it goes. The following chart is an analysis of splits from our 400 free relay at prelims for the State Meet in 1999. The same four swimmers set the State record in the finals.

Name	Time	Strokes/Lap				Total Strokes
		Lap 1	Lap 2	Lap 3	Lap 4	
Whistler	53.17	14	17	17	18	66
Wolbert	55	14	18	19	20	71
Thayer	54.79	14	17	18	20	69
Galloway	54.08	12	16	16	18	62

There is a range of six strokes between the highest and the lowest counts, and I have no means of ascertaining if these were optimum ranges in terms of statistically validated analysis. Random counts on the last lap of other swimmers in the same heat were in the 22-23 range.

The counts on the first lap are obviously lower because of the start. I think that our kids tend to have counts that are lower than most swimmers on this lap, because we spend so much time working on maintaining speed off of the start. I also think that the huge amount of time we devote to turn work and streamlining in addition to stroke efficiency causes our kids to have lower counts.

It is important to note that each swimmer selected her own rate according to what *she* felt was necessary for the circumstances. We had done a tremendous amount of controlled swimming with prescribed stroke rates during the season, but at the end of the year, it was left entirely up to the swimmers. As the race progressed and fatigue set in, each swimmer increased her count to compensate for diminishing distance per stroke.

I just read a biomechanical study of the 2001 Olympic Trials that made recommendations for improving performances in different strokes and distances. It seems that distance per stroke is not as much of a clear-cut indicator for success in swimming as has been found in the past. For the women, the recommendations called for developing increased stroke rate in distance free, back, and breast. Male freestylers in all distances and female sprint freestyle should work on distance per stroke.

These findings are for elite athletes, and it would be interesting to compare their stroke lengths with those of non-elite swimmers. I would guess that there would be a significant difference.

If I were coaching elite swimmers and coaching all year long, I would give much more emphasis to developing their ability to be efficient at higher stroke rates. However, I feel that swimming at higher rates comes naturally, so we need to continue to focus on DPS as our primary goal. I will have to take a serious look at including more sets at higher rates in the future.

Fueling the Fire

We are getting near to championships, and it is time for more focus on championship thinking. I read a great deal on sport psychology over the summer, because the mental aspects of our races seemed to be a weak point for us last year during championships. In the book *Competitive Fire*, Michael Clarkson makes a fascinating point that out of the top 100 all time greatest athletes, most had a serious crisis in their early lives that seemed to fuel the fire to achieve. Many athletes at the elite level use rage about criticism, either real or imagined from competitors, media or coaches to propel them to great feats.

In my experience, at this level, we have much more success by focusing in our own lanes while being aware of what competitors are doing. I think tapping into anger is a very risky strategy, because in most cases, it leads to over-arousal and distracts the swimmers from focus on the race.

Our athletes seem to be much better off focusing on the task at hand and cultivating a sense of flow, not on winning and losing. The idea is for a competitor to improve his skills by meeting the challenge provided by a skilled opponent.

Csikszentmihalyi , author of *Flow* says, "Competition improves experience only as long as attention is focused primarily on the activity itself. If extrinsic goals such as beating the opponent, wanting to impress an audience, or obtaining a professional contract — are what one is concerned about, then competition is likely to become a distraction, rather than an incentive to focus consciousness on what is happening."

I think that the great amount of technique work we do is a huge advantage in a meet like conference championships. Muscle memory seems to compensate and kick in when the mind and body are fatigued. Before prelims, we talked about what a big advantage we have over other teams, because we can compensate for fatigue by using better technique.

The Good, the Bad, the Ugly

In football, you have to win a few ugly games in order to have a great season.

Prelims were definitely ugly, but our kids got the job done. On the plus side, a number of kids hit lifetime bests, and at least three kids in every event made either prelims or finals. On the down side, our best kids looked truly awful. I knew they would, and I knew when I gave them the 20 x 100 with the fly finishes that it would take a lot out of them, and we have always had our better kids swim through this meet, and they were tired because they were swimming at 9:30 at night after being awake since 5:30 am, and, and, and….

The fact is that even though the rational side of me was prepared for this, it was still hard to watch. I do a great deal of second-guessing and rethinking what we have done during the season and wondering if everything was a mistake. Fortunately, history is on our side and we have always rebounded and swum well in finals.

This year's finals were a startling exception and I don't know why. The good news is that we won championships by over 100 points over second place. The bad news is that we were awful from the medley to the last relay. We were the spit valve on the big trombone of life; we had a total of one good swim the entire meet. What bothered me more than anything about it was that we looked incredibly sloppy in all aspects, especially turns. We lost focus for the first time this year.

I have to think that it is the result of having so many kids who have been here and done that before. We had a regular practice on Friday between prelims and finals. We didn't rest, taper, or shave for this one, and the message was that it was not that important. Still, there is never an excuse for swimming sloppy, especially in light of the huge amount of time we had spent on these aspects of swimming.

I felt especially bad for the kids who needed this meet to make Sectionals and didn't. All of them missed chunks of the season for one reason or another, and in a short season, a week of practice missed is going to hamper results. It is very difficult to set team priorities that meet every swimmer's needs.

For our team, the focus has always been on the Sectionals and State meet. There is not enough time in the season to prepare for three big meets. It is hard to say to the team that this is a stepping stone meet where we get a chance to race and then say to four or five kids, "Oh yeah, and you guys have to go fast." I would hope that the lesson these swimmers would take from the experience is that they need to set their sights on Sectionals next year.

I was very impressed by Eric's and Doug's teams at the meet. Both teams had been struggling early in the year, and these guys did what great coaches do — continue to work with the team regardless of the talent level. For a lot of coaches, the "rebuilding year" is a lame excuse, but for both of these guys it was exactly what they were doing. Both of their teams looked entirely different than when we swam them during the dual meet season.

The biggest upside of the meet was that, once again, I got to hang out in the coach's room with the homemade chili and other goodies while my friend Eric, "the diving guru," watched his *four* divers.

A Romantic Gift

While I was hiking this morning with my friends Geek and Paulie, I was contemplating how my better swimmers could be having such irrational fears and anxieties after being so successful. Paulie reminded me of the first time he took me mountain climbing.

He told me he liked to go climbing in the Adirondacks and asked if I wanted to go along with him. It sounded like a great idea, so we went in the wintertime. (The Adirondacks are exactly like the Himalayas, except that Mount Marcy is five miles lower and not as steep; yet, for me, they present a serious challenge).

When Paulie and I went for the first time, the weather was horrendous. There was rain, snow, sleet, and every other type of weather possible. As we approached the summit, there was a raging blizzard and we were literally crawling on our hands and knees. I happened to be the one at the front when we did reach the summit. I could tell because everything dropped off.

Just as we summited, the snow stopped and I could actually see where we were. Paulie was delighted and was savoring the view. He was encouraging me to come over and look at the view from the edge of the cliff with him and noticed that I had retreated into the fetal position and was trying to find something to hold on to. When he asked me what was wrong, I simply replied, "I don't like heights." Paulie thought I probably should have mentioned it before we got to the top, but it didn't bother me as long as I couldn't see where I was going.

I have since made about a dozen more trips up various mountains, and still experience abject terror every second I am above the tree line. Still, I love going, because the company is great, there are no mosquitoes when it drops below zero, and we only spend a brief time at the summit.

For many years, when my wife asked me what I wanted for a present, I told. Her response was that if she bought me one of the gifts I wanted, I would just get into a situation where I would get hurt. She relented last Valentines day, and I got the romantic gift every man craves — an ice axe.

The next day, I went out to Hitchy's and we proceeded to test it out on a frozen waterfall. I ended up with a large hole in the back of my leg about the size of the pick end of the ice ax. The official version, which Hitchy swears to, is that I hit a stick that just happened to be that size.

The reason I wanted the ice ax all along was that it would ease the terror I feel every time I go near a peak. This year on the trip up, I was far less anxious. I felt so much more comfortable knowing I had the ax with me, even though I had to ice the hole in my leg the whole way up in the car, and when we got there, there was over six feet of snow on the ground. I left the ax at the lean-to when we went climbing, as it would have done us no good in those conditions.

My experience must be like that of some of my better swimmers who are doubting themselves. They have been to the summit of high school swimming by winning at the State meet, and yet they somehow are afraid of the return trip.

I know my fear of heights is entirely irrational, as is the idea that an ice ax will make me safer; yet, it doesn't affect the way I feel.

I guess I just have to figure out what will act as an ice ax for them.

One of the details from *The Perfect Storm* that impressed me when I read it was the way that ocean going vessels are designed to be self-righting if they are capsized. I am sure that this team is similarly constructed. We have two weeks of uninterrupted practice for Sectionals and another week for States.

Practice of the Week – Week 10

Warmup Set: 4 x 100 IM

LA: Hand lead kick

SA: Swim with maximum of 6 spl

At least 5 dolphins off the wall for FL and BK

Swim 8 x 50

1st 25: Easy BK, max speed turn with at least 5 dolphins off the wall

2nd 25: 12_ sprint free and 12_ easy

Swim 8 x 25 in heats

Odd 25's: 20-yd sprints from the blocks @ max speed and Stroke Rate

Even 25's: When all heats finish 20-yd sprint, choice of drill back

Drill for 10 minutes: choice of drill – I'm confident the swimmers know what they need at this point, but I still offered suggestions for those who wanted them. I had no takers which is good.

Swim 8 x 50 in heats @ Max speed from the blocks

Drill (of choice) 1 x 50 between each fast 50 for recovery

Swim all 8 fast 50's in same stroke

Our kids who have not yet qualified for sectionals did only 2 of these 50's and then worked with Deb on starts and turns. I'll give them an off day tomorrow as they need to go lifetime bests to make it back for finals.

We finished with 10 x 50 drill/swim choice. I reminded them how important it is to do the drills perfectly to reinforce great technique when the neuromuscular system may be fatigued. This is important for two reasons: 1) To condition the system to dealing with the accumulation of lactic acid, and 2) To focus the mind on what to do to compensate for the pain and effects of fatigue. Otherwise it just becomes something akin to ferret legging.

WEEK 11

The Superintendent and the Snowbank: Good Observations, Bad Interpretations

I was thinking about the conversations I had with Paulie yesterday, and I started to laugh out loud. I usually do that when I am around him; he is a great tonic for whatever ails a soul. He is also one of the reasons I am slow to make assumptions about kids.

Paulie and I taught together in a shared room at school for 6 years, during which we had lots of emotionally disturbed kids. Somehow, we didn't have much of a problem relating, and generally had a great time.

I knew he had graduated from Orchard Park a few years before I got there, and during a snowstorm, I told him the story about how the year before I started teaching, some whacko kid had jumped out of the 3rd story library window and into a snow bank.

Paulie told me that he had indeed heard the story as well, and had some inside information. He proceeded to tell me that he went directly from the snow bank to the principal's office to a 5-day out of school suspension, but had enriched himself by almost five dollars from the other guys at the lunch table.

Telling Geek some battle stories from our days teaching together, Paulie and I talked about teaching little kids in the summer program. One of the stories centered around one of our all time favorite kids, Ryan. Ryan was a kind, gentle, guileless, beautiful kid who could tell nothing but the truth. Paul was trying to teach him the concept of more and less, so he set up some real world problems. He would say, "Ryan, if you could choose either three tootsie rolls or 2 rocks, which would you choose?" Ryan would choose the rocks. Paul would patiently change the problem to include increasingly more aversive objects in the less category and increasingly greater amounts of candy in the more pile; Ryan would always choose whatever was presented in the less category.

After about the third day of this, Ryan calmly said, "Mr. Connelly, I know what you are trying to teach me. I understand about more and less, but I don't like candy."

It was a classic case of a kid exhibiting a particular behavior and an adult making wrong conclusions as to the reasons behind the behavior.

Oh yeah, I forgot to mention that Paul, the nut case kid who jumped out the library window and who was told by his guidance counselor that he shouldn't even think about going to college, is now a school superintendent pursuing his doctorate.

I was greatly relieved when I talked to the kids about our abysmal performance this weekend. I told them how dismayed I was to see them swim so poorly when I knew how much they had put into their season.

A couple of them pulled me aside and confided in me that they just didn't care about the meet. They were sore and tired and knew that they were going to win no matter what; they just wanted to get it over with and get home. They didn't want to hurt my feelings and say anything at the meet, especially in light of the fact that one of our team goals for the meet was to act positive no matter how we were feeling. They guaranteed me they would be in the warrior princess mode when it came time for the Sectionals and States. It was a classic case of a kid exhibiting a particular behavior and an adult making wrong conclusions as to the reasons behind the behavior.

I had planned a tremendously challenging traditional workout for the day, because I figured that if they were having doubts about their conditioning, completing a mind numbingly hard series of workouts this week might give them more confidence. This workout was not conceived as a punishment in any sense of the word. I never use practice as a punishment, because it sends the wrong message. The kids know that, to me, practice is never a reward or punishment, it's just our means of getting better performances.

If there is a great physical challenge involved, it is because I feel it is a necessary one to aid in the process of swimming faster.

Anyway, I pitched that workout and came up with a practice on the spot. I figure that technique had gotten us this far, and we might as well dance with the one that brung us.

Today in my Global 9 class, we were talking about Chinese philosophies and how they shaped Chinese society. We began to talk about martial arts such as tai chi, which is connected with Taoism.

Although it is thought of as a gentle and meditative form, in actual combat conditions, Tai chi is one of the most lethal of all the martial arts. Tai Chi incorporates slow speed patterning of *perfect* movement through 360 degrees of body rotation, stressing balance and core body movement. My teacher demands that each basic movement be perfected before moving on to the next one. My understanding of the thought behind it is that the neural pathways are grooved so that in a true performance situation, there is no conscious thought to interfere with the speed of perfect movement.

Tai Chi has been around for a few thousand years, so I trust they've had a chance to work some of the bugs out of the basic principles. Even the little bit of study I have done has taught me the concepts of balance, core body movements, leverage, and the extreme value of relaxed strength, which I've seen described as steel wrapped in silk. For me, the greatest challenge was to become relaxed sufficiently to gain the fluidity of motion that my instructors demanded. These are concepts that have existed in various forms for millennia. It almost seems like the wheel had to be reinvented to move these concepts into the water. (My limited experience with tai chi which made me able to throw my former offensive lineman mutant son around like a rag doll. I can write this because he doesn't read stuff without lots of pictures to color).

A typical example from the classic text, *The Tai Chi Treatise*, ties in with the emphasis on continuing flow in swimming:

Continuing and Flowing Movements

The "outer academies" use clumsy external strength, so that the beginning and the end are broken. The opponent thus has the chance to attack. Tai Chi emphasizes the mind instead of force. From the beginning to the end, it is continuous without interruptions, like an endless circle. As the "Tai Chi Treatise" has said, "As the long river and big ocean, flowing ceaselessly." It has also said that applying jing is "like pulling silk from the cocoon." This describes the importance of continuity.

Great swimming is like the long river and big ocean, flowing ceaselessly but with great power. This emphasis on continuing and flowing movements is critical in good swimming. We have traditionally emphasized the power end of strokes that produce a surge and then a dead spot where the enemy, in the form of resistance, has a chance to attack. Great swimmers produce strokes that have surges of power as waves in the ocean, but their strokes are more continuous and without interruption to achieve a higher *average* velocity, so the enemy has fewer openings for slowing forward momentum. The great swimmers indeed look like they could "pull silk from the cocoon." At this point in the season, this is the kind of sensation we should be approaching in the water.

The "outer academies" often emphasize jumping and bouncing, which spend much strength. After practicing, one will naturally be short of breath. Tai Chi practice emphasizes calm and peace of mind to overcome vigorous movements. Although they move, they are calm and tranquil. It is best to practice as slowly as possible, because when the movements are slow, breathing will be naturally deep and the chi will sink to the lower dantien (midsection or body core). The learners will understand by thinking deeply and continue practicing it for its purpose.

Again, there is much similarity in approaches. "Human" swimming makes water an adversary. In this mode, the goal of a good workout is how short of breath swimmers are at the end of a set where much strength has been spent unnecessarily on overcoming resistance. Masters of "Fishlike" swimming are more adept at using the water instead of fighting it. To accomplish this, it is best to practice at slow speeds with a great emphasis on natural breathing. The midsection is a focal point of all movements in fishlike swimming.

Thinking deeply and practicing at slow speeds are cornerstones of both Tai Chi and Total Immersion. It is only after the essentials have been mastered that higher speeds are attempted.

Tai Chi practiced without a teacher will provide benefits such as relaxation and flexibility, but will not provide the same benefit as it would with a teacher pointing out the intention of the movements. When my teacher explained that the opening movement was done as a block to keep an opponent from kicking me in the groin, it took on an entirely different level of importance.

It is my understanding that most martial arts operate in a similar manner, in that the teacher gives his students his undivided attention at all times. It is inconceivable that any martial arts teacher would simply post a workout and tell his students to "go do 20 Tai Chi forms on two minutes" while he went off to sip green tea and read the paper. Such a scenario should be equally inconceivable for swim coaches. A martial arts teacher would never give instructions to go and drill without a providing the student with a focus on a particular aspect or aspects of performance. So should it also be in swimming.

One of the things that fascinates me about the martial arts is that I know a number of black belts in different disciplines, and not one of them has ever used their martial art for its intended purpose. The question then arises — why would they spend countless hours for years and years when there is no end product?

The answer must be flow.

I had a girl come to the pool in near hysterics because her grades were below 90. I was a little less sympathetic. I told her that I spend my day with kids who work for hours and hours every night just to pass. When she calmed down, we talked about some strategies she might employ to improve her study habits and improve her grades.

It continues to baffle me that the most accomplished students and athletes on the team are the ones who express the most self doubt and seem the most emotionally fragile when it comes to dealing with competition in either of those realms.

Ted Turner has said, "Motivation for superachievers is a complex subject, but it goes back to some degree to a sense of insecurity... that because they're insecure, they're always trying to achieve, trying hard to show they're good persons, and that they're successful." It seems many parents are trying to provide the motivation to super achievement by pushing hard instead of supporting.

A friend of mine sent me an email this week about the difficulties one of his best swimmers is dealing with.

At prelims, she showed some emotion for her swims for the first time since I have known her.

She was crying and I asked her, "What is making you sad?" She said the time upset her. I asked her why she cared all of a sudden when she has admitted to not caring (or enjoying one second of swimming since she was ten years old.) She quickly stopped crying and said, "you're right, why should I cry?" To me, the tears showed that she does care on some level...she is just not sure what level. She has a neurotic parent who pressures her and pushes her well past her breaking point. At finals I responded to her question of "what do you suggest I do for the 200 race, Coach?" with a simple answer, "just smile before, during, and after the race as the other girls on the team will benefit more from that than you being upset for some undetermined reason." As it turns out, she swam better than I had seen before. She looked like a weight was lifted off of her back and she was allowed to enjoy the experience. And her swim helped to propel the other swimmers to better swims.

Today, I spoke with her again. As it turns out, her parents were not at the meet...something that I thought would never happen. I asked her if she thought that was a factor...at first she said no, but seemed to be fluctuating on second thought. Hopefully they will be out of town from now on.

We are experiencing an epidemic of parents who are living vicariously through the exploits of their kids, and making their lives miserable in the process. The sports sections are rife with reports of fans in almost all sports abusing referees, coaches, opponents, each other and their own kids during competition. My Australian AFS student was telling me that Australia is experiencing the same epidemic. I don't know what it is about my generation of parents, but we have collectively lost perspective on sports. For some reason, far too many well-intentioned people my age have gotten their egos involved in the success or failure of their kids, and it is making kids crazy.

In my initial writing of this chapter, I wanted to include my impressions of the only parent of an Olympian I have ever met — Gene Mills. I was privileged to spend some time with him on more than one occasion, and got to ask him about how he raised Glenn. It became immediately clear that Gene and his wife provided an atmosphere of high expectation and discipline tempered with unconditional love and support. The push to achieve came from Glenn. Unfortunately, Gene passed away as I was working on this book, and I thought it would be more appropriate to use Glenn's own words about the world's best swimming parent. Gene carried his parenting skills with him when he changed careers and became a coach.

A Tribute to TI Coach Gene Mills

By Glenn Mills

The best part of coaching is the chance to enrich and empower swimmers and students. Countless kids were blessed that Gene Mills decided to spend his last years coaching and teaching swimming.

For 27 years, my father made his living as a pension insurance salesman, and as a manager. He worked very hard, and made many friends of co-workers and clients. The honest insurance man was the way I described him.

About nine years ago, I sat down with my father, figuring that someone who sold pensions for a living would no doubt have a good plan set up for himself... and he did. When I asked him why he was continuing to work so hard when he could be living in easy retirement, he said simply, "What else would I do?"

At the time, I was coaching an age-group USS team in downtown Cleveland, and I offered him a job coaching with me. I explained to him that coaching was a lot like public service — for not much pay, you got the privilege of everyone telling you what you were doing wrong. But I assured him the rewards would be vast. I knew this from my own coaching. My Dad knew it from the experience of having three sons involved in swimming. It was a sport that had brought our family great joy, and had pulled us through some tough times, especially after my brother Kyle died. My Dad was convinced. Within a couple months he had made all the arrangements, and submitted his resignation.

The stories I'd like to share with you came to light within the past week. My Dad passed away on Monday, January 7th 2002, and these are just a few things that have happened to me since.

When I arrived in Cleveland on Monday evening to be with my Mom, she informed me that on Tuesday night we were going to a swim meet. The team for which Dad was assistant coach was having a meet. They had dedicated their season to Dad and had invited us to share in their commitment to honor him. It turned out to be senior night, where each of the senior swimmers was introduced, and then marched out with his or her parents. Each senior read a short story plus a short personal message to his or her parents. The whole ceremony was very touching. Then the team asked my Mom, my brother, his kids, and me out in front of the audience. Someone read a beautiful dedication message, which captured the heart and spirit of my father. Then the swimmers walked out, one by one, to greet each of us with a hug. Each swimmer presented my Mom with a red carnation with a personal message attached to the stem. These kids were preparing for a swim meet, yet they'd taken time to do this. The parents in the stands were in tears and, of course, we were, too.

As one of the swimmers, Steve, walked past me, I saw his T-shirt for the first time. On the back was a picture of my father. I called Steve back to get a closer look, and the words across the back of the T-shirt read, "If better is even an option, then good is not enough," — Coach Gene Mills. And underneath was printed… This one's for you, coach.

Through the evening, as we watched the meet, people kept coming up to us and sharing with us how our Dad, and husband, had touched their lives. Swimmer after swimmer, parent after parent, spoke about his unselfish commitment to ALL the swimmers, not just the best ones, and the way he tried to help each kid, every day. They talked about the way he kept swimmers in the sport through a soft hand, and yet how he seemed to know when to be stern and demanding with the ones who were slacking off. They talked about how he cheered for kids who didn't even swim for him.

I had thought my Mom was joking when she asked me to go to a swim meet the day after her husband — my Dad — had passed away. I didn't really want to go, but then I thought about all the meets my Dad went to for me, when he probably didn't want to go. I thought about how he would work all week, then spend hour upon hour driving, then sitting in the balcony of a hot pool, just to watch me perform for what was, hopefully, as short a time as possible. So in the end I went, we went, we stayed for the entire meet, and we wouldn't have missed it for the world.

Two days later, at the memorial service, several people who had attended the swim meet approached me and told me how they saw my father in me, especially as I cheered for swimmers I didn't know. They told me how much that meant to them. I explained to them that it was nothing more than knowing how lonely it is in that pool. It was also that I knew my Dad loved these kids, and therefore I loved them, too. It was as simple as that. If they thought I was in any way like my father, I felt humbled to the core, but I know I have a LONG way to go to be like my Dad.

During the week, an old friend who is coaching in Indiana wrote me a letter when he heard about Dad. A friend of his had sent him some messages being posted on the Internet about Dad. High school kids were posting messages on a discussion group, and they were writing short memories and dedications about my father. Just to give you an example of what was being posted, I'll pick out a nice one and share it with you:

Not Forgotten

Re: Gene Mills aka Mr. Mills (Avon Lake Swimmers)

Date: Tue, 08 Jan 2002 21:08:04 GMT

From: His swimmer <unknown>

People die everyday, and life goes on. But Mr. Mills wasn't just a person. He was more then a person. He wasn't just a husband, a father, a grandfather or a coach. He was our coach. Things like this don't happen to people like him. Every day when we would go to swimming he would be smiling that smile...you couldn't forget it. He would ask you how your day was, and if you said anything but GREAT, he wouldn't let you go. You had to tell him you were having a wonderful day. If you asked him, "Mr. Mills, how are you?" he would respond with "Great, but things will pick up," or "Today is the best day of my life until tomorrow." He cared about everyone, from the Olympic hopefuls to the kids who can barely make it down the pool. At swim meets he would walk up and down the pool yelling. If you weren't on our team he talked to you and asked your name. He was the friendliest person. There is now a hole, a hole in our team, and a hole in our hearts that can't be filled. On January 7th we lost someone that we can't replace. He might be gone but he is not forgotten! This one is for you, coach! We love you!

These were high school kids, who learned so much — not just about swimming, but about life — through my father. I couldn't have been more proud, yet, at the same time, more sad.

At my Dad's memorial service, I stood in the reception line to greet more than 400 people. At one point, a little girl with long beautiful hair peered up shyly at me and said, "Your Dad made swimming fun." It was such a simple statement, yet the devotion and love in her young voice brought tears to my eyes.

She had exactly captured the essence of my Dad, her coach. I looked down at her and said, "My Dad made everything fun." As I reached out my hand to shake hers, not wanting to scare her with a hug, she walked past my hand and embraced me with such firmness that I could feel her emotions. This girl couldn't have been more than 11 years old, yet she could have knocked me over with her love for my Dad.

Her father went on to tell me about the link between my Dad and his daughter — about how she couldn't wait to get to the pool to see him. She thrived on his smile, his warmth, and his ability to teach her things. Because of his knack for turning every lesson into a victory, no matter how small the improvement, she felt successful every time she swam for him. It was just plain beautiful.

Many young children attended Dad's memorial service with their parents. One in particular came up to me and said that my Dad had taught her how to swim freestyle. The family then told me about their other daughter who, even though she had a disease that prevented her from swimming, couldn't wait to go to the pool with her sister. She loved how my Dad always made a fuss over her even though she couldn't participate in the lesson.

I explained to the little girl that the things my Dad taught her would be with her all her life. That's when it hit me that this is his legacy. His legacy isn't me, necessarily, or my brother or our children. It's all these little kids who will swim beautiful freestyle for the rest of their lives, and who have a love for the sport that my Dad helped to instill. I can only hope that Gene Mills's swimmers will be swimming until the year 2100 and beyond. These kids were young. It could happen!

The little girl's mother talked to me at length about my Dad's teaching process, and I explained to her that Dad and I had found Total Immersion at the same time, and learned the process together. She said that, week after week, she sat through the lessons wondering when all this was going to come together. She wasn't able to see or understand the entire process, but then it happened. When it all came together, the mother understood, and was thankful that her daughter had such a patient teacher, who waited until her daughter was ready to move on, rather than go by a preplanned timetable.

Through the course of the evening, another man approached me and told me that he had met my father through Love, Inc., a charity that supports needy families in the Lorain County suburb of Cleveland. He said that he remembered one meeting in particular when Dad showed up with a whistle and stopwatch hanging from his neck. The man had laughed and asked if he was going to a costume party afterwards... he looked the epitome of a coach. Dad explained that he WAS a coach — that he taught swimming in Avon Lake. The gentleman, who had three young daughters, started to put two and two together, and asked Dad if he knew one particular young girl who was gaining a reputation in the Cleveland area for her beautiful swim strokes. Dad smiled and replied, "She's one of my students." Within a couple of days, the man had moved his daughters to swim for my father. This man was so taken with my Dad's simple teaching process that he began to teach it to kids at his local health club. He is having so much fun that he's even expressed interest in becoming a professional swim teacher.

As far as swimming is concerned, I just kept thinking what lucky parents these were to have a man with this level of commitment teaching their kids. A man whose only interest was the swimmers, and not his own. This kind of outlook on the sport had a great effect on the swimmers; they actually WANTED to go to swim practice. They learned something new at each practice, they were rewarded with encouragement and acknowledging words, and they felt a sense of accomplishment each day.

My Dad never worried about yardage, long workouts, or hammering out the intervals. Yet he produced beautiful, fast swimmers — and kept them coming back to the pool. He made sure they loved the sport and were proud of their efforts. He not only taught them great strokes, but also helped them to be great people.

I'm grateful beyond words to have had a father who taught me so much about being a man, a father, and a coach. Our time together was way too short, but I'm thankful for every moment, because he had a way of making every moment count. From what I saw last week, many other people are thankful, too.

I have only 15 kids in the water now and a perfect opportunity to teach, but nothing left to teach them. I have over coached at this point in past years, and the results have not been good. At this point, there should be nothing but minor tweaking going on, and certainly no attempt made at increasing fitness levels.

As Caesar said, "*alia iacta est*" — the die is cast.

I am confident that I will finish the season with a few less holes in me than Caesar did at the end of his.

Practice of the Week – Week 11

Pre-Warmup: 2 rounds of 8 widths in heats from a pushoff

Round 1: At least 3 dolphins, then max speed/power underwater kick to wall

Round 2: Max kick to breakout, then ez to wall

Before Round 2, we did two minutes of relaxation breathing with no talking. Then we did breakouts with eyes closed. I got this idea from Scott Lemley, the creator of Fistgloves. The point of the exercise is to eliminate visual stimuli and become more aware of the kinesthetic cues involved in the breakout process.

Warmup set: (with small fins and Fistgloves)

4 x100 IM

Odds: Kick on SA strokes and drill LA

Evens: Hand lead kick on LA strokes and choice of drill on SA strokes

Swim 8 x 50

1st 25: At least 4 dolphins to BK breakout, then swim ez BK to flags

2nd 25: Max speed turn-and-breakout then ez FR to wall

Swim 8 x 25

Odds: From blocks @ max speed to "touchpad" finish @ flags (not wall)

Evens: Drill of choice.

The reason for practicing finishes at the flags is so they can get used to lunging forcefully without worrying about jamming fingers, and maybe breaking some of those Homecoming fingernail specials.

Kick/swim 1 x 400

Odd 25: Fast hand lead LA kick

Even 25: LA choice ez swim

Kick 8 x 100 on 2:00

Descend 1-4 and 5-8, from ez to max speed

Take off Fistgloves and fins.

Swim 20 x 50 FR on :45

This was intended as a relaxing recovery, after the intense kicking sets. Just stay long and make the intervals.

Swim 1 x 800 IM/FR

Odd 25's: Fast stroke in IM order

Even 25's: ez FR @-3spl

We used two lanes for each group, going fast stroke down one lane and returning ez FR in another to swim perfect race form down the middle of the lane.

Cooldown set: 8 x 50 Drill/swim SILENT

Odd 25: EZ anchors

Even 25: ez FR @–3spl. Focus on good anchor on both lengths

WEEK 12
Almost There

Perspective

I did a presentation with my Global class on the differences between Renaissance and Medieval art. One of the greatest differences is that the renaissance artists benefited from the discoveries of an architect name Bruneleschi who discovered perspective through scientific and mathematical analysis. Prior to this discovery, no matter how much effort an artist put into his painting, it would still be essentially two-dimensional in appearance. The works of the most talented were the most lifelike. With the discovery of the techniques of perspective, anybody could make basic three-dimensional representations of the world on a two-dimensional surface. However, the discovery of perspective did not relieve the artist of a great deal of hard work. Creating a masterpiece was still going to require an investment of time, concentration, and diligence, and ultimately, it was the talent of the artist that separated the great from the very good ones.

On the Eastern side of things in Global 9, we were discussing philosophies that have shaped Chinese history. Three of the principles were Taoism, Legalism, and Confucianism. Taoists believed in following "the way," which reveals itself to those who are open to it, and that the natural order of things will reveal itself; therefore, a minimal number of rules are necessary. The Confucianists believed that if people are educated about a well-defined core of basic values, a series of relationships based on mutual responsibility will make for a society that will be orderly, and there will be little need for coercion to enforce rules. They also believed that the leader should lead by example. The Legalists believed in rigid adherence to rules. Any deviance was severely punished to make an example of the offender, but good conduct was lavishly praised and rewarded. They all had in common a reverence for teachers; especially swim coaches, who were just below the emperor in standing.

China experienced periods of great prosperity under the leadership of emperors who embraced these philosophies. It also experienced upheaval and chaos when leaders forgot that the welfare of the people was paramount, and ruled in order to increase their own status and comfort.

It struck me that most coaches I know could be categorized as holding philosophies that fall within the range of these three.

I have seen tremendously successful coaches who have virtually no rules. I have seen coaches who have very elaborate and specific codes of conduct who likewise succeed. I have also seen abysmal failures who have let chaos reign or who have developed rules and a system of punishments and fines so elaborate that neither they nor the kids understand it.

To me, it seems that successful adopt a wide variety of philosophies that are comfortable for them, but ultimately about what is good for kids. Coaches who adopt measures that are convenient for themselves and use the success of their swimmers to bolster their own egos may have periods of success, but are doomed to ultimately fail.

I think that I have adopted a more Taoist orientation as I have gotten older. I find little need to either reward or punish behavior, as I feel that if a kid is not seeking "the way" to better swimming, I cannot help her.

I think the successful coaches are the ones who adopt a philosophy based on what is comfortable and natural for them and, ultimately, live by it as the way to do what they believe is best for kids.

One of the most difficult things for any coach to overcome is a tendency to spend more time with the fastest kids. I have worked hard to avoid this, but I get to know the kids who qualify for the most challenging meets so much better. With successively more demanding qualifiers, our numbers drop each week of post season. It's so much easier to communicate with a group of 16 than with a group of 30, although the added rest seems to make the smaller groups feel compelled to make enough noise to fill in for those kids who aren't moving on to the next level.

For some reason, since we have switched to a more technique-oriented approach, we have had great tapers. This was easy to explain when we just pounded on the kids and then let up, as the body super-compensated. What mystifies me is that our kids tend to swim best times or close to them during the season and then have large drops at the end. I am much more accustomed to kids swimming poor times all season and then having the drop.

This was especially apparent in 1997, when our pool was down for the season. We had less practice time each day and far fewer practice days, yet we swam great at Sectionals and even better at the State meet, when I was sure we would run out of gas.

Sectional prelims went very well for the most part. The kids showed a great deal of enthusiasm and most did what they needed to do to get where they needed to be in finals. Most of our veterans had a great attitude and got the job done, and the attitude rubbed off on the newer kids.

We did have some poor swims, but only one of them was unexpected. Many times, we see that kids who have to swim their best at Conference Championships tend to fall off a bit when they get to Sectionals. There is just not enough time to peak for two meets.

One of our seniors had a terrible meet. She has had difficulty dealing with the pressure of competition in the past. We have worked hard to improve things through mental toughness exercises, but they proved to be largely ineffective.

This is the type of situation that genuinely dismays me.

Some of our poor performances were due to illness, and in a very few cases, not doing the base work that makes a taper successful. However, in this case, the athlete has done everything I have asked and then some, and it really bothers me that I can't help her find the key to unlocking her vast potential.

The problem is that she is a senior and was part of the relay that finished second in the States last year. Both of us desperately wanted her to be a part of that relay again, and she knew that team policy had been that the fastest four swim, except with seniors. Seniors on our team are honored for their commitment by being treated as the heavyweight champs. Relay spots are theirs to lose, and in order to unseat the champion, there has to be a knockout punch, not just a tenth or two. So far, she was taking a standing eight-count.

At school, we talked at length today in an attempt to relieve some of the pressure on her. She is a very muscular kid, and she may just need more rest. We decided that if she did not swim well in her event at Sectional finals, she would not swim in the relay but would be able to swim at State prelims.

One of the other seniors had broken the no crying rule on deck at prelims. She had not made the time to come back to finals and couldn't hold back the tears. She did, however, follow protocol and went to the locker room to cry.

She came to see me at practice today to let me know that she wasn't crying because she swam poorly. She wanted me to know that she "wasn't being a sissy." The realization that her career on this team was ending was a sad experience for her. It was for me as well. I told her I understood, because beautiful women have always wanted to be around me as much as possible. It's just an effect I have on them and I can't help myself.

We both laughed, and I don't think she noticed my eyes were watering a bit. I must have been reacting to the high chlorine levels in the air at that moment.

I have seen tears like hers before in a very unlikely place.

When my son was 10 he was hit by a car. He had a skull fracture and a broken leg, and almost didn't pull through. When we were finally allowed to see him in the hospital, I asked him how he was doing. His reply was "not too swell." That was the only complaint he made during a rehab period that had to seem eternal for a 10 year old; he barely cried.

One of the reasons we have a close relationship is that we have spent a lot of quality time together in various emergency rooms when he or I, or sometimes both of us, broke things and had to get stitches. He never complained about pain.

This same kid cried his eyes out when his football team lost their championship game his senior year. It had nothing to do with losing. It had everything to do with the realization that there wasn't a huge call at the next level for offensive linemen who weighed 160 pounds. He knew this was the end of the road for him and that he would never again put on shoulder pads and be part of a team that meant so much to him.

One of the reasons that the Chinese Empire went from being the most advanced and powerful empire in the world to being subjugated by a handful of Europeans was an overzealous adherence to traditional education. Chinese scholars did not deem math and science to be worthy of study. The Chinese emperors developed a strong case of ethnocentrism, and decided that anything that did not originate in China could not have much value. As a result, the Chinese became so bound in tradition that they missed out on developing technologies that could have enabled them to resist European imperialism.

This book makes little mention about swimming science. One may get the impression that I don't think it has value. In actuality, I am acutely interested in biomechanics, conditioning, nutrition, and physiology. I read everything I can get my hands on by Doc Counsilman, Ernie Maglischo, and Phil Maffetone, and have had extensive conversations with Bud Termin, who does research at the University of Buffalo. The reason I hardly mention the science is that there are many more sources that are far more authoritative, accurate, and detailed about these aspects of swimming.

In my Global class, we talked about the Scientific Revolution, which had its origins in the Renaissance period, which was a time when scientists, such as Galileo, challenged just about every notion people had about their world and their place in it.

The established method of scientific inquiry in Galileo's time was to consult existing texts and find out what the ancients, such as Aristotle, had to say about the subject at hand. Galileo and others like him thought that theories should be tested through experimentation. It was far more comfortable for many to rely on dogma.

Galileo ran into some very stiff opposition when he started to question the Aristotelian stance the church subscribed to. Professors of philosophy who believed that only spherical perfect bodies could exist in the heavens scorned Galileo's discoveries. Galileo felt that interpretation of the Bible should be adapted to ever-increasing knowledge, and that no scientific position should ever be made an article of faith.

It seems that some in the swim community have taken up the role similar to that of the Aristotelians. The doctrine they hold onto is that harder swimming and big yardage is the only way to create speed. They seem to feel that anything new of any consequence is merely a gimmick or a con, and heap scorn on novel approaches, simply because it's not the way swimming has always been done.

The laws of physics tell us that water is a medium 887 times denser than air, and offers exponentially increasing resistance as the speed of a body moving through it increases. Might we see speed gains as a result of cutting down resistance and swimming more efficiently rather than increasing power? Heresy.

It seems to me that strict adherence to one particular dogma in swimming is not going to yield the best results.

Artist Coaches

I just purchased *The Swim Coaching Bible*, and read the chapter from Mike Bottom, "Freestyle Sprint Training." It focuses mainly on the development of energy systems in training sprinters, but I was impressed most by his conclusion:

> As a coach-artist, I judge my success by looking at each individual as a piece of art, and I urge you to do the same. Each athlete is in fact a work of art in progress. If you gear programs to the masses you may develop swimmers who produce — but

you will not be a successful coach until you can refine your techniques for each individual. Each canvas can reflect your work, and you can be proud of what you create. If a season passes and you are not satisfied with your work on a particular canvas, maybe more red, white, or blue is needed: maybe more green, purple, gold or platinum will help in another instance. The exciting thing is that you are the artist. There is no blame involved in creating: the only consideration is the result. Take responsibility for your artwork and enjoy the process.

As a younger coach, I watched what successful coaches I knew did and mirrored my program after theirs. I would go to clinics, get workouts from the most successful coaches in the world, and have my kids do them. What I failed to realize was that in most cases, these coaches were dealing with elite athletes, and, in the case of college coaches, physically mature athletes who had had years and years of training. It didn't dawn on me that kids who swam for three months out of the year might not benefit as much from aping this type of training

I was always much more interested in the conventional ideas presented, but patiently sat through presentations by a strange man named Bill Boomer anyway. I think he is the swimming world's version of Galileo. Many, including myself, scorned his ideas until they were legitimized when Olympic coaches Richard Quick of Stanford and Eddie Reese of Texas gave Boomer free rein to work with their teams.

I have seen some of the workouts that Eddie's swimmers do; they are multi-dimensional in terms of the kinds of challenges, but there is no way around it — they involve a tremendous amount of very hard work. I see him as the epitome of the artist-coach.

The artists of the Renaissance embraced findings of scientists such as Galileo. For example, they incorporated into their paintings renderings of the moon as it was seen through Galileo's telescope.

Eddie is a coach who I try to emulate. I love his presentations at clinics, because he is a genuine Renaissance person in that he is much more than a one-dimensional thinker. When I heard Eddie speak a number of years ago, he started off by saying he had just finished a very profound book called *Ishmael*, a book that didn't have anything to do with swimming. It was about a gorilla. I went home and bought the book and found it to be one of the most profound books I have ever read. I have about six copies of the book now that are floating around with colleagues, family, friends, and students. I have yet to have one of them tell me it didn't make them think in a different way about the world we live in.

One of the things that also makes Eddie a Renaissance person is that he is constantly experimenting. One year, he showed tapes of his sprinters doing dryland on scooters that they were laying on and propelling themselves down the halls with their hands. The kids were having a ball.

Renaissance people were humanists. One of my coaching friends had a kid who was being recruited by Eddie a number of years ago and went down to talk with him. What impressed him the most was that Eddie didn't talk much about swimming; he talked about elk hunting. A number of people who have watched Eddie's practices are always struck by the fact that he makes a personal acknowledgement of every swimmer in his pool at every practice.

It seems to me that most of us would fall more to one side or the other on the scientist/artist continuum. Recognition that coaching is not entirely one or the other is essential for coaching success.

When I got to school for the bus ride to finals on Saturday, the kids were laughing and joking around with each other. When we got on the bus, I told them I wanted quiet, and to my surprise they gave it to me — for a few seconds. I pointed out to them that there was a lack of seriousness and a lot of laughing going on and that if they wanted to ride on the bus with me, they were to keep laughing and enjoying themselves and do the same when we got to the meet.

It has been my experience that guys need more quiet, intense focus to swim well. With the girls, I have found that they perform best when they are loose and relaxed. I make it a point to be likewise on deck, even though I am tremendously anxious. I tell jokes, goof around with the kids, and give them one piece of information, such as, "Make sure you hold your streamlines." I told our breaststroker, who would be in the most competitive race of the day, to focus on increasing rhythm and driving with the hips in the final surge to the wall. I also spent a great deal of time teaching her to deal with the press. I told her that after she won, the first thing she was to say to any reporters was, "My coach is not just a pretty face. He knows stuff."

While the playoff football game that our school played in last night had over 6000 spectators, I would be surprised if there were more than 10 people in the stands at Sectionals from Orchard Park who did not have kids in the meet. There is no pressure on me in the public arena, as there is on my friends Geno and Bobalone who coach the football team, yet I always feel a tremendous sense of relief when our kids have a good meet.

It is a dynamic that I haven't come to grips with, but even after all of these years, I still feel my pulse elevating and my heart pounding in my chest before races. I have come to realize that it is due in part to the tremendous pressure my swimmers put on me by being as attentive, dedicated, and hard working as they are. When you are the leader of a group that religiously follows your instructions, the mirror is the only place to look for someone to blame if things don't pan out.

Fortunately, we had the finest Sectional meet we have ever had. We won all three relays and three individual events, despite the fact that our four fastest kids have not shaved yet. Our medley swam in a different order than we will use at States, because the kids were confident that they could win and I thought it would be a big psychological edge for the kids to go into the State meet knowing that we can drop a full second by switching our flyer and freestyler. The relay went 1:50.88, and the kids have to drop a little over a second next week to break the State record, which has been their goal since the start of the season.

One of the highlights for me was that our sprinter, who had been struggling, took advantage of shaving and rest to go over a second faster than she had in prelims, solidifying her spot on the 200 free relay. I hope she translates my faith in her into faith in herself for the State meet.

I once again was delighted that I didn't have any divers. I got to enjoy the hospitality room, which had that great combination of traditional Buffalo fare — chicken wings and pizza. I'm sure the pepperoni and wings were tofu-based and, therefore, low cal and cholesterol-free.

I must make another offering to the powers that be to send me no divers. I hope they will accept the pizza crust I left for them in the spirit that I offered it.

Practice of the Week – Week 12

"Instead of holding a bow taut while holding it straight,
   better to relax.
You may temper the sword until it is razor sharp,
   but you cannot preserve the edge for long."

-Lao Tzu

Warmup set: with Fistgloves

Swim 4 x 100 IM

Focus on "slippery" side-swimming for LA and Silent swim for SA

Kick 8 x 50 LA

Odd 25: No-kick pushoff for max distance, then kick ez

Even 25: Max pushoff and max-speed kick

Swim 8 x 25 Descend 1-4 w/Fistgloves and 5-8 without

At this stage, every length we do is to sharpen the racing edge, the primary focus of our taper.

Swim 4 rounds of 4 x 75

LA strokes as follows:

- 1st 75: 25ea: @-3,-2,-1spl

- 2nd 75: 25ea: 5/4/3-cycle burst, then ez

- 3rd 75: 25ea: –2spl, max. speed (any stroke count), -2spl

- 4th 75: 25ea: Drill/Swim max/Drill

SA strokes as follows:

- 1st 75: 25ea: SA combo swim 3-3/2-2/1-1

- 2nd 75: 25ea: 5/4/3 strokes max burst

- 3rd 75: 25ea: KickEZ/Swim Max/Swim EZ

- 4th 75: 25ea: Drill/Swim max/Drill

The focus of this set is to intersperse some fast swimming with relaxed and long movement to experience speed without fatigue.

Swim 5 x 25 from blocks. Max speed to 12 _ then ez.

Focus on great breakouts and relaxed starts. Deb worked with the Medley Relay on relay exchanges. She has a knack for visually "freeze framing" fast motions like starts and relay pickups much better than I can.

Cooldown: 1 x 300 choice with a focus on Flow

Notes: At this stage, I give almost exclusively positive feedback and rarely comment on anything needing correction. By now, I feel they must swim with the patterns they've developed and memorized. I'm 99% satisfied with the quality of their technique, so it's essential to get them focused on sensing what they are doing well and simply honing their sense of smoothness, seamless breathing, streamlines and breakouts.

It's often critical to resist the temptation to over-coach in the final week. The swimmers need to be ready to get up and swim as automatically as possible. Now is not the time to try to convert a 2-beat kicker to a 6-beat kick.

Ends and Means

*"We have perhaps a natural fear of ends. We would rather
be always on the way than arrive. Given the means, we
hang on to them and often forget the ends."*

-Eric Hoffer, U.S. philosopher, Reflections on the Human Condition

---

From the Buffalo News:

**Lehner, Rubin, Belke score double wins: Swimmers
advance to state meet**

By Mary Jo Monnin

News Sports Reporter

11/11/2001

Robin Lehner won the race of the day by swimming the race of
her life on Saturday.

The Orchard Park sophomore used a furious kick at the end to
come from behind and win the 100-yard breaststroke in 1:06.93
to cap an eventful day at the Section VI Swimming and Diving
Championships.

The sectional meet at Erie Community College's Burt Flickinger
Aquatic Center was also a qualifier for the state championships
at the same pool next weekend.

"I was totally surprised," said Lehner, who transferred in May
from Arvada, Colo. "I looked at the last 25 yards and noticed I
was a little behind, so I knew I had to catch up. All I wanted to
do was get in the top four."

The breaststroke field was so competitive that senior Allie Dean of Kenmore West, freshman Jamie McGowan of East Aurora and sophomore Kelly Stoklosa of West Seneca all hit the magic time (1:09.23) needed to qualify.

The win in the breaststroke was the second of the day for Lehner, who earlier won the 200 individual medley in a personal-record 2:11.17. Lehner said her 36.72 split in the breaststroke leg allowed her to hold off runner-up Ginger Miller of Frontier, who qualified for her fourth states in 2:13.51.

Lehner was joined by seniors Rachel Rubin of Amherst and Stephanie Belke of Sweet Home as double winners.

Another swimmer who will be thinking Section VI record next week is Orchard Park junior Martha Whistler. Whistler couldn't have come any closer to the mark in the 50 free as her time of 23.89 fell just short of the 1985 record of 23.88 held by Barb Bolton, also of the Quakers.

"The key is the start. For me I have to get off and get out and get ahead early," said Whistler, whose trip to states will be her fifth.

It was no surprise that Orchard Park swept all three relays. The foursome of Alaina Thiel, Lehner, Marie Wolbert and Whistler won the 200 medley in a season-best 1:50.88. They'll be shooting for the Section VI record of 1:50.28 next week. East Aurora's all-freshman relay team also qualified.

Thiel, Whistler, Stephanie Furlani and Wolbert combined to win the 200 free relay in 1:39.75. Lockport's Jourdan Spark, Karissa Tolli, Maren MacDonald and Lauren Yacos swam a school record 1:40.61 to qualify its first relay team for states in at least 20 years.

The 400 free relay of Whistler, Thiel, Samantha Turner and Wolbert, won by a gaudy 9 seconds in a timed final.

It occurred to me today that I haven't used a watch in practice on more than a handful of sprints this year. I'm going to keep it in my pocket. Most of the times that I have, it's been to satisfy my own curiosity, and I've rarely shared times with the kids. It seems to me that the kids get much more out of working on their own subjective sensations of speed and smoothness, and I can always find positives about each swim without having to fudge times.

Also, I noticed that our backstrokers and flyers were using their legs too much on their breakouts. We took them separately for a few reps of 10-second vertical dolphin bursts with an emphasis on *body driven* fast rhythm and relaxation. I always make the kids smile when they do this because it relaxes them more. Then they did a few widths underwater to polish things. I told them to make sure they did some of this at warm-up for States.

Relay Pickups

The medley relay is set in terms of who is swimming what, but I've still not decided who is swimming and in what order in the free relays, so during practice, we first work on starts for the medley, then change the rotation for free relay start practice so the swimmers get used to starting off different people. We have to focus on being more aggressive. Until now, I've been reluctant to have the kids be too aggressive, because we haven't practiced enough. However, if we are going to be competitive, aggressive starts are a must. Everyone is in agreement that if we get called for a jump, it's bad officiating.

During a conversation that Robin and I had about her breaststroke race, I imparted the type of advice I give swimmers at a championship meet. Rather than focus on what the other swimmers would do, it was important to give one strategy that she could focus on and would give her control over what she was doing in the race. It was going to be decided in the last lap, as four swimmers were among the top in the state and separated by one second. We talked about the need to change to a faster rhythm in the last half of the 4th lap and to make sure that her tempo was torso-driven and not arm-spinning. Again, Robin was able to incorporate it and come from a body length behind to win.

Music, like my stopwatch, was largely absent at practice during this season. We used to play music all practice long. We would play loud fast music for the swimmers, and we used to play Mozart for the divers to help them with their concentration. I felt that music was a good way to help the swimmers take their minds away from swimming, to ignore the pain; this was when I felt that enduring pain was the biggest part of good swimming.

It slowly dawned on me that I was creating an atmosphere like the shop owner who employed the mechanics who butchered repairs on author Robert Pirsig's motorcycle in *Zen and the Art of Motorcycle Maintenance*:

> They sat down to do a job, and they did it like chimpanzees. Nothing personal in it. There was no obvious reason for it. And I tried to think back into that shop, that nightmare place to try to remember anything that could have been the cause.

> The radio was a clue. You can't really think hard about what you're doing and listen to the radio at the same time. Maybe they didn't see their job as having anything to do with hard thought, just wrench twiddling. If you can twiddle wrenches while listening to the radio, it's more enjoyable.

However, once we made the commitment that we were going to emphasize technique over all other aspects of swimming, we had to ditch the music. Great swimming has everything to do with hard thought. If it's going to be a flow experience, it must be autotelic, and be an end in itself. At first, it was difficult for some to go without the music, but now the only time anybody mentioned music was to get psyched up for a meet. Mindless wrench-twiddling is no different than mindless swimming. The job gets done, but not with any quality. If we are going to do a quality job, swimming demands 100% of our attention and focus. Dissociative swimming is a thing of the past.

If the mechanics had worked on Pirsig's motorcycle with the same diligence, care, and focus that my swimmers have in their jobs this year, he never would have cause to reflect on the poor maintenance job; and hence, he probably wouldn't have written the book, and I wouldn't have had a chance to enjoy it as much as I did. I'm glad the schleps did the job.

Similarly, Pirsig wrestles with the concept of quality.

Quality...you know what it is, yet you don't know what it is. But that's self-contradictory. But some things are better than others, that is they have more quality. But when you try to say what quality is apart from things that have it, it all goes poof! But if you can't say what quality is, how do you know that it even exists?

It is appropriate that I don't know how to explain what I have seen this year in terms of the volume of quality I have seen. Terms like flow, grace, rhythm, speed, power, relaxation, ease, etc., can't really begin to describe what has transpired in the pool. I can't begin to adequately describe it, but *I* know it existed.

Old Folks Boogie

I went for a walk in the woods with Gus. Hitchy couldn't go because of a serious back problem. I know hanging out with me doesn't help him much. I guess he must be getting old. As the Little Feat song goes, "You know that you're over the hill when your mind makes a promise that your body can't fill."

It made me wonder about when it's time to hang it up. How do you know when you've stayed too long at the dance? I just know that the last thing I want to do is coach "because I don't know what else to do," a quote that I recently heard from a coach who should have retired years ago. This same coach walked into a locker room of athletes who had just given their all and were devastated at having lost a meet due to an official's error and said, "I'm not used to losing" and walked out on the kids. It ruined *his* win-loss record.

A journal entry from 1998:

> *My daughter's soccer coach, Tom Cashmore, has been a friend of mine for a long time. I was so pleased that my daughter would have the opportunity to learn from him — he's the kind of coach that every parent wants their kid to play for, a genuine role model.*
>
> *Tom has been battling Hodgkin's disease since he was in high school, but he has never let it get in the way of enjoying life. He teaches adaptive physical education and every person who has come into contact with him professionally or personally raves about what a class guy he is.*
>
> *At the start of the season, my wife, who works with Tom's wife Karen, came home with the news that the doctors he had been working with for the last two decades had given him the word that there was a new mass present and that they were powerless to do anything about it. They told him to go to Sloan Kettering hospital for a second opinion, but were not optimistic.*
>
> *Needless to say, I was devastated. I had lost two close friends already that year, and chose to believe that it would not happen again. Tom was going to be OK.*
>
> *I didn't say anything to my daughter, because I knew he would have his own way of handling things, and didn't want to interfere with the process.*
>
> *Tom told his kids on the first day of practice that the doctor had given him 4 weeks to live and that had been 6 weeks ago. He planned on coaching the full season, but would miss some days. It was that important to him. He gave the message loud and clear that if he heard anything about anybody "playing for Mr. Cashmore" that he would resign. He said, "There's only one reason to play soccer or any sport — because you love it."*
>
> *Tom had promised the kids he would be at the big game of the season no matter what, but he had to go to Sloan Kettering*

again. Everybody at the game was ill at ease when it started with an assistant on the sideline.

It is hard to describe the elation when he showed up midway through the first period with news that what they had thought was a new inoperable mass was scar tissue.

As I write this, Tom is still coaching soccer as intensely as ever and is in great health.

"Because you love it…" The great coaches always know it's not about them.

I have enough experience to know how little I know, and at this point in my career, I have too many unanswered questions and theories to test out to entertain any notions of retiring in the foreseeable future, but I need to give some thought to recognizing the signs that will tell me it's time to go.

It seems to me that after the great Sectional meet, there is little that could happen to improve on the season. It's been such a great time getting to this point that I'm ambivalent about the fact that this is it until next year. Anything that happens from here on in is a huge bonus.

Being able to get our four fastest kids unshaved into the State meet was uncharted waters for us. I know physics are involved in the shave, but the psychological edge of knowing we got into the thick of things with all three relays unshaved must be big.

I am hopeful that if things stay true to form, most people at the State Championships meet will go slower than at their Sectional meets. This is because in such a short season it is difficult to maintain an edge when most sections have a league championship and State Qualifier meet prior to the State championships. This might give us some edge, because, in theory, staying sharp with a technique-based program should be easier than with a training base. If technique has been the primary focus of the season, a swimmer is more likely to have a great race, regardless of how precisely the taper has been managed. It's not as dependent on hitting a peak on precisely the right day. That's the theory; I'd still be more comfortable if it was fact.

We went down to the meet pool to practice for the last time and then go out for pizza. The lanes were extremely crowded, so I just let the kids do what they felt they needed and pretty much left them alone. I gave a few focal points to some of the kids, but did no timing at all on anything. Some of the kids told me what they had done and asked if that was enough. I asked if they felt good, they said they did, and I said that's enough then.

To some watching, it might have appeared that I was indifferent to what my swimmers were doing during this time, as I genuinely pay little attention. My swimmers know better. Before we left practice yesterday they asked what we would be doing for practice tomorrow, and I told them it was up to them. I would be happy to give a workout or suggestions if they wanted or felt they needed it. I had no takers. They knew that there is no better way that I can demonstrate my confidence in them than to say, "You know far better than I what you need, so go do it."

We needed to do some relay pickups when they were ready. I told them that the only thing they couldn't do was full-length sprints, a pretty radical departure from past practice at a big meet. I told them to limit any fast swimming to a 3- or 4-cycle burst so that they could save the good stuff for tomorrow.

Deb did the relay starts with the kids as I watched from a distance. I was impressed by the spring and explosiveness off the blocks, which I hadn't seen since the first days of practice. That, coupled with the laughter and easy banter on the trip in and on deck, told me that the taper was taking and that they were ready to go fast.

I was delighted and a bit nervous to see that the Johnson City 200 and 400 free relays made it to the States. Jim did a great job with them.

One of the genuine scholars on our staff told me that in France after World War II, workmen were repairing the roof of one of the cathedrals and discovered a fabulous stained glass window that had been placed there by the glassmakers guild as an offering to God where nobody would ever behold its splendor. It was a window of incredible beauty and there was much debate about what to do with it. Should it be brought down and incorporated in the cathedral or put on display at a museum? The decision was made to honor the offering of these craftsmen and cover it back up.

I sit here wondering how this is all going to pan out, and I am confident things will go well. The people who crafted this fine season did so out of pride and not for the recognition. I am also confident that no matter how we do, the season will be a masterpiece of devotion, skill, and sacrifice that has already been covered over. This too is as it should be.

Imparta l'arte, e metitila da parte — learn the art and then put it aside.

Prelims went well for us. We were first in the Medley Relay and second in the two Freestyle relays. Ironically, the team that is ahead of us in the 200 Free Relay was Johnson City. Jim and Chris had obviously gotten the message across to their kids. I was excited for them.

I knew the 400 Free Relay was going to be a tough one for us. Newburgh beat us in prelims and broke our state record in the process. I also knew our kids would give them a serious run at finals, using a different order. In prelims, Robin had to go from winning the number one seed in the breast to the relay with only one heat in between. She did a great split, but would have at least 20 minutes between events at finals. I hoped that would make the difference.

Whenever I go out to Hitchy's with Gus, we almost always see wild turkeys. I'm not a hunter, but my hunter friends tell me how cagey, cunning, and difficult they are to find, let alone shoot. I never go looking for them, but almost always run across them. I have literally hit them on my mountain bike. It seems that many of life's experience are like this. If we seek too hard, what we are looking for eludes us.

Our team goals, which we had set at the onset of the season, included winning all three relays at the states and breaking the state record in the medley relay.

Finals started off on a high low note. While we won the state title in the Medley Relay for the fourth consecutive year — an amazing feat considering that 10 different girls participated in that streak — the kids did not break the state record. I had talked so much about them getting the record that the kids became focused on the peak and forgot about the journey. It is not an accident that I have so much patience with the slow learners that I work with during the day.

The photographer who tried to snap a picture of the elation of winning a state championship must have been perplexed. He was behind the blocks right after the race, and I heard him say to the girls, "What's wrong, didn't you just win the State championship?" Their faces were wrought with disappointment about not getting the record.

Maybe some young guys out there can do better then me, but when I play with my stopwatch, the best I can ever do starting and stopping is about .12. That was the difference between us sweeping the relays as we set out to do and finishing second twice.

We lost the 200 Free Relay by one-one hundredth of a second. The great thing is that Stephanie was able to overcome her doubts and fears and swam the race of her life to keep us close.

The breaststroke was deja vu all over again. The same three girls from Sectionals went 1,2,3, only this time, Robin went 1:06.33 instead of 106.93.

Robin is extremely shy and quiet, but she pulled off one of the all time best "gotchas" anybody has ever pulled on me. The swimmers in the championship heats were marched out and introduced. They had filled out brief biography cards that were read as the swimmers got on the blocks. When it was Robin's turn, the announcer read the part about her being the Section VI champion. Then, there was a pause and the announcer said, "She would also like everybody to know that her coach is not just another pretty face."

My wife was in the stands and I hope she took note. I get tired of just being an object.

The 400 free relay, which I had considered to be the longest shot to win, was definitely the race of the day. We had four fabulous swims and broke the state record. Newburgh also had four fabulous swims and broke the state record, only by 11-hundredths of a second more than we did. It was inspiring for me to see our girls hugging the winners for their great effort.

Last summer, I bought a new "Lemond" road bike. I had always had pretty good bikes when I raced, but never anything like this marvel of technology. I wrestled with the idea of getting a triple chain ring, but sense won out over vanity.

One of the things I do really well with the 50 pounds I have put on since I last raced bikes is ride downhill really fast. While riding, I had come to a long, steep descent and was watching the speedometer go from 35 to 40 to 45 to 50. It was exhilarating until I hit 53 mph and the bike started to vibrate violently. I knew from years of experience that the last thing to do was to tense up and hit the brakes, so I relaxed and feathered the brakes. The bike began to slow, and I had a great deal of time to contemplate how I was going to hit and roll when I crashed in order to minimize the damage when I hit the pavement, and also to think about the large volume of flesh that I would be leaving on the road.

Eventually, I miraculously came to a stop and stayed upright. I got off the bike and checked for loose parts; maybe the headset or a wheel skewer had been loose, but I found nothing. When I got home, I again checked and found nothing.

I asked the guy I bought it from why it had acted like that. He said that he had no idea, but why the hell was I going 53 mph anyway? I asked numerous other people, and the best explanation was "harmonic vibration" — if one of the wheels was a few millimeters outside of true, at that speed it would start a vibration that would amplify as it sent itself through the frame.

We might have had a harmonic vibration of sorts in an otherwise well-tuned machine. Then again, through all of the diligence, attention to detail, and hard work, the kids may have eked every millisecond possible.

It is hard to explain why I left the pool with an overriding sense of disappointment. I felt that with the talent level and unparalleled commitment and focus of the team, we should have won everything. I have told my kids over and over again that these things do not guarantee success. It's precisely because of the unpredictability of the outcomes that sports are such an important part our lives.

I've been around long enough to know that outside recognition of accomplishments in swimming will always be minimal. When I look at the grand scheme of things, I always start off with the fact that there are a billion Chinese people who have never even heard of Orchard Park High School. There are people in my own school who don't know that I coach swimming. I also realize that in light of world events, first or second at a swim meet is of paltry significance, especially after talking to a coach from New York City whose swimmers compete in a pool just outside of Ground Zero.

All of America has struggled to determine what is important in our lives and where our priorities are. I think the pursuit of excellence in any of its forms must benefit us all, and that, even in light of catastrophic events, it still has a vital place in the lives of these kids.

I guess an ending where everybody succeeds is too much B-movie fare, and this is the real world. I think what I am feeling is that a perfect ending would have been just right for this group, as the season has been as close to perfect as would be possible for any team. I hope the kids have gotten a fraction of the pleasure from the experience that I have, and I could never begin to thank them enough for all they have given me.

Glossary of Terms used in Practice examples:

FR, BK, BR, FL: Freestyle, Backstroke, Breaststroke, Butterfly

4 x 100

LA…

SA…

This is a standard warmup. LA refers to what the swimmers are to do on the BK and FR. SA refers to what the swimmers are to do on the FL and BR.

DPS: refers to Distance Per Stroke. This indicates an emphasis in the set on increasing Stroke Length.

LA: Long Axis — a set of skills common to freestyle and backstroke, in both strokes the body rotates along the spine — or 'long axis' of rotation.

SA: Short Axis — a set of skills common to butterfly and breaststroke; in both strokes the body rotates around the hip-to-hip — or 'short axis' of rotation.

Spl: Strokes per length. Stroke count per length of the pool.

Head Lead: Any balance or rotation drill done with both arms at the sides.

Hand Lead: A balance or rotation drill done with one or both arms extended.

Silent: Swim or drill with the least possible noise. One of the favorite technique focal points among Total Immersion coaches.

@-2 spl: Two strokes fewer than your usual count or fewer than a benchmark count established in the set. -3 spl is three strokes fewer.

3, 4, 5, 6- cycle bursts, then ez to wall OR 6, 5, 4, 3- cycle bursts, then ez to wall: Swim 3 (or 4 or 5 or 6) cycles of the whole stroke at maximum speed, then ease off. The goal is to swim with complete efficiency and fluency while ALSO swimming at maximum Stroke Rate. A highly valuable form of nervous system training to remain efficient at sprint racing speeds, without the fatigue or muscle breakdown of lactate-type training, because no lactic acid is produced in these short bursts. The EZ (easy) swimming should also be done with impeccable form.

2-ct, 3-ct: Hold a glide in extended position or in Sweet Spot for 2 deep breaths or 3 deep breaths.

Drills: Slide & Glide, Body Dolphin, Skating, UnderSwitch, ZipperSwitch, OverSwitch, etc.: Drills are all illustrated on Total Immersion videos. See resources appendix for order info.

Resources

On-Line Help

www.totalimmersion.net

The TI website offers no-charge support and information as well as an on-line Learning Community for coaches, swimmers and all who are interested in or curious about swimming. Important features include:

- *Total Swim*, a free newsletter featuring immediately useful articles each week, in the same thoughtful, inquisitive style used by Art in this book.

- An on-line Discussion Forum for swimmers and coaches. Use this forum to share your insights, discoveries and successes, to ask questions and to tap the experience of others who are teaching or coaching in the same way as outlined in this book.

- New video clips weekly, spotlighting key refinements of TI drills and skills.

- Regularly updated samples of TI-specific practices for both technique improvement and effective training.

- Information on how YOU can become a certified TI teacher-coach. With the huge demand for TI instruction on all levels, becoming a certified TI Teaching Professional is one of the best ways to increase your income potential – and is also an enormously satisfying way to hone and use your professional skills.

Total Immersion Self-Help Tools

TI offers books, videos and DVDs that distill the complex movements of swimming into simple concepts and progressions that can help *any* swimmer achieve satisfaction and maximize their potential. TI books, videos and pool tools are fully guaranteed. If at any time you're not absolutely satisfied, contact TI for a full refund AND you can keep the book or video. For complete information, visit **www.totalimmersion.net** or call **800-609-7946 or 845-256-9770**.

TOTAL IMMERSION VIDEOS

FISHLIKE FREESTYLE: The Total Immersion Way (released 2002)
This 58-minute video illustrates all the Freestyle drills used by Orchard
Park HS swimmers. Organized into six easy-to-follow lessons featuring
Shane Gould, the best freestyle swimmer in history, plus other TI swimmers demonstrating the 14-step learning process for Fishlike Freestyle
exactly as taught at TI workshops.
$39.95 VHS or $44.95 DVD

BUTTERFLY AND BREASTSTROKE: The Total Immersion Way
FREESTYLE AND BACKSTROKE: The Total Immersion Way
If a picture is worth a thousand words, a great instructional video is
worth 10,000 words. These 45-minute videos were designed as companions for *Swimming Made Easy,* providing clear images and complete instructions for short and long axis drills. Key points are shown
in slow-motion and underwater views. $29.95 each

TOTAL IMMERSION BOOKS written by Terry Laughlin

SWIMMING MADE EASY:
The Total Immersion Way for ANY Swimmer to achieve
Fluency, Ease and Speed in ANY Stroke.
SME provides exhaustive guidance on applying the principles of Total
Immersion to all four strokes. It also includes the step-by-step learning
methods for developing each stroke via TI stroke drill sequences in 10 lessons, illustrated with 150 surface and underwater photos. Ten chapters
on skill development show you how to swim with the efficiency and
fluency of elite swimmers. $19.95

**Read a free sample chapter at www.totalimmersion.net/
products/140chapter.html**

Fistglove® Stroke Trainer: Using the Fistglove® Stroke Trainer with
TI drills and training techniques will increase your body awareness in
the water and help you swim fluently and efficiently. $9.95 each or call
or email for team prices.

TRIATHLON SWIMMING MADE EASY: How ANYONE Can Succeed in Triathlon or Open Water Swimming
While the title refers to Triathlon Swimming, this is really a comprehensive guide for how to swim freestyle with confidence and mastery at any distance and in any body of water. Part 3 offers detailed guidance on how to teach and practice the drill sequence illustrated in the *Fishlike Freestyle* video. The 10 chapters in Part 4 include the most complete description ever written on how to transition from: simple drills, to advanced drills, to whole-stroke swimming, to swimming *fast*. $24.95
Read Chapters 1 to 3 at www.totalimmersion.net/tsmechap.html.

WATERPROOF, LAMINATED POOL PRIMERS:

FREESTYLE and BACKSTROKE: the TI Way:
BUTTERFLY and BREASTSTROKE: the TI Way:
These are the perfect companions to our four-stroke videos: The Long Axis Pool Primer illustrates TI drills for Free and Back. The Short Axis Pool Primer illustrates TI drills for Breast and Fly. Both are spiral-bound, laminated and waterproof. Place them right on the deck at the end of each lane as a guide to the key points of TI drills and techniques for each stroke. Buy them risk-free for $29.95 each.

HANDS-ON COACHING FROM TOTAL IMMERSION

For those interested in receiving help directly from certified Total Immersion coaches, we offer the most effective swimming instruction on earth.

TI Team Workshop: Give us a weekend and we'll teach your team and coaches what *really* matters in swimming.
Would you like every swimmer in every lane of your pool to swim significantly better…immediately? Would you like your coaches to have the ability to teach "Fishlike Swimming" while other teams practice wasteful "Human Swimming?" A Total Immersion Team Workshop is the most cost-effective and time-effective way to introduce your entire team to excellent swimming. When applied to an entire team and coaching staff, Total Immersion will produce visible improvement from Day One, and establish foundations for excellence that will carry forward for years to come.

Contact info@totalimmersion.net and ask for an information package to be sent to you.

TI Weekend Workshops: We'll Teach You To Swim Better Than You Ever Thought Possible!

A TI Weekend Workshop is the most transforming swimming instruction available anywhere. Our students realize immediate and dramatic improvement after just a few hours of our specialized instruction. And for coaches, the ideal way to learn how to *teach* TI technique is to learn it in the water first. We routinely work miracles with unskilled and inexperienced swimmers. And even if you think of yourself as a pretty decent swimmer, we guarantee you'll be far more fluent and efficient after two days. Experienced and accomplished swimmers tell us they learned more in two days of TI instruction than in 10 years of traditional training.

Write terry@totalimmersion.net for more info.

TI Teacher Training: Let Us Teach You To Be One of the Best Swimming Teachers on Earth!

Thousands of swimmers are asking where they can find a Total Immersion teacher. We offer 3- to 7-day programs of intensive training in all three forms of Total Immersion Instruction. These include:

Learn to Swim: How to teach non-swimmers the balance skills that will allow any student to progress to fluent swimming in any stroke. LTS training will also include training in the Gruneberg Method, which will allow you to help someone with paralyzing fear of the water to be comfortable enough in the pool to successfully complete LTS lessons. GM has successfully cured a lifetime of fear in as little as two hours and is an enormously valuable adjunct to your LTS teaching skills.

Fishlike Freestyle: Learn how to teach the skill progression taught in TI weekend workshops.

Different Strokes: Learn to teach the simple, effective skill progressions for butterfly, backstroke and breaststroke.

Write terry@totalimmersion.net for more info.

Notes

Notes

Notes

Notes

Notes

Notes

Notes

Notes

Notes

Notes

Notes

Notes

Notes

Notes

Notes